Carrier's Kitchen

Robert Carrier

B🌿XTREE

GRANADA TELEVISION

First published in Great Britain by Boxtree Limited

Text and photographs © Robert Carrier 1995

The right of Robert Carrier to be identified as Author of this Work has been asserted by him in accordance with the Copyright, Designs and Patents Act 1988

1 2 3 4 5 6 7 8 9 10

Designed and typeset by Geoff Hayes
Photography by Michelle Garratt, except for pp 32, 125, 152 by Jack Nisberg, pp 49, 68 by John Stewart, pp 81, 105 by Pipe-Rich, p. 104 by Paul Webster, p. 144 by Cy Gross, p. 168 by Martin Brigdale, and p. 189 by Eric Morin.

Printed and bound in the UK by Bath Press Colourbooks for

Boxtree Limited
Broadwall House
21 Broadwall
London SE1 9PL

A CIP catalog entry for this book is available from the British Library

ISBN 0 7522 1032 7

Front cover photograph by Paul Webster

Contents

Introduction

The trendy style magazines have been filled with lush colour spreads of barely refurbished beach huts, outhouses and 'minimalist' decors for more than a year now. A bare new look for a jaded new age: scrubbed or painted floors, sanded and distressed furniture, a cottagey look for sophisticated city dwellers. Tricia Guild's *Painted Country* book did much to crystallise this new movement with its bright colours, its freewheeling style and its basic good sense. That clinched it for me: my new kitchen in my Suffolk cottage, set happily between a lush vineyard and an ancient wood, would be Carrier Country. So welcome to *Carrier's Kitchen*, home base for a series of television cooking lessons on Granada Television's 'This Morning' programme.

The kitchen boasts a 30 foot scullery for food storage, refrigeration and larder facilities, an auxiliary gas range and oven and – most important of all – my specially designed Cook's Prep Cart. This invaluable item has a smooth wooden surface for making cakes and pastry and open shelves below to store baking and pastry making equipment.

The kitchen itself is really two rooms – a family-style dining area complete with a large round maple-topped table and deep comfortable armchairs for conversation, reading and just plain relaxing. The cooking area is dominated by a large gas-fired cooking range imported from France, with a professional high-fired gas grill that can sear fish, steak, chops and poultry to savoury highly coloured perfection in a matter of minutes, while leaving the centres as moist and tender as one could wish.

Perhaps the most unusual feature of the new cooker is the smooth-topped centre cooking plate (just like in a restaurant kitchen) which allows the cook (me) to start off a pan of water at the centre for a quick boil and then, simply by sliding the pan to the outside perimeter of the solid steel surface, let it continue cooking at the lowest simmer.

The third fitment on the cooktop is a built-in deep-fryer. This is large enough to cook chips for the whole family but small enough to allow me to deep-fry in minutes small batches of *beignets* (French style fritters); *pommes soufflés* (delicate souffléd potato chips that puff up before your eyes) and wonderful crisp-coated cheese tidbits with deliciously creamy centres. All without fuss or bother, frying odours, or bringing out special deep-frying equipment.

If you have seen my moveable Cook's Cart on the programmes, you'll know that this specially-designed mobile cooker is also a moveable centre island, complete with chopping block, extendable wings and a four burner gas hob (fed by a Calor gas canister safely hidden from view inside the unit). Thanks to this cart I can finish cooking a dish in the centre of the kitchen while other dishes simmer away on the main range; bring the unit to the table to cook with my guests; or wheel it out effortlessly on to the terrace for outdoor meals with style.

With such a comfortable, yet workman-like setting, it is no wonder that the television crew and I have enjoyed creating the special dishes for the series. In the following pages I share with you my special techniques and recipes for grilling, pan grilling, stir-frying (great recipes for pan-fried and stir-fried vegetable dishes on pages 110 and 118) and roasting. I also introduce you to the professional cook's method of composite cooking (starting a dish on top of the stove, then finishing it off in the oven), the professional chef's trick of the trade which guarantees you superbly grilled, pan-grilled and pan-fried steaks with succulent, moist centres. The Composite Cooking lesson (see pages 151-157) also shows you how to effortlessly prepare sauces and butters for a dish as you cook it . This first series of programmes ends with a lesson on *en papillote* cooking (cooking in a 'paper bag' made of parchment, kitchen paper, or aluminium foil). The second series of ten programmes includes the quick techniques of Chinese Steaming, Deep Frying, Pot Roasting, Cooking With Wine, Success With Vegetables and Cakes and Pastries.

My thanks go to Tim Hopewell and Dominic Santana, my brilliant directors on the programmes, to Annie Stark who was with me in the kitchen throughout the series, providing the back-up dishes and making sure I had the right spoon for each shot, and to my gifted editors at Boxtree, Charlie Carman and Penny Simpson who made sure I crossed my Ts and dotted my Is. They made it all real.

I hope you have enjoyed the series as much as we have filming it; and that this book of recipes will bring new enjoyment and expertise to your cooking.

Bon Appetit ... from Carrier's Kitchen

Robert Carrier
September 1995

Simple Starters

French 'composition salads' – *salades composées* – make wonderful first course or luncheon salads for spring and summer meals. The procedure is simple: just toss your chosen salad ingredients, raw or cooked, in a well-flavoured vinaigrette dressing (1 part wine vinegar or lemon juice to 3 parts olive oil, ½ level teaspoon Dijon mustard and salt and freshly ground pepper, to taste). Add chopped fresh herbs or flavour with finely chopped onion, shallot, garlic or crumbled cooked bacon.

Salade Italienne

Lettuce leaves, crisp rings of fennel, sprigs of fresh fennel and stuffed green olives. Vinaigrette dressing.

Salade Mexicaine

Cos lettuce leaves, canned corn kernels and red pepper strips. Vinaigrette dressing flavoured with mustard and finely chopped parsley or chives.

Salade Japonaise

Lettuce leaves and sprigs of watercress, garnished with radishes cut into flower shapes. Vinaigrette dressing flavoured with finely chopped garlic and soy sauce.

Salade Fermière

Lettuce leaves (Salad Bowl) and sprigs of watercress, garnished with tomato wedges and quartered hard-boiled eggs. Vinaigrette dressing flavoured with mustard and chopped onion.

Salade Provençale

Lettuce leaves and barely cooked florets of cauliflower, garnished with black olives and anchovy strips. Vinaigrette dressing flavoured with mustard and chopped garlic.

Salade Gitane

Chick peas, lentils and *haricots blancs*, soaked overnight and then cooked separately in water until just tender (you'll need three separate pans); each tossed, separately, while still warm, in a vinaigrette dressing flavoured with chopped onion and anchovies. Garnish with tomato wedges and black olives.

Salade Paysanne

Lettuce leaves, sliced mushroom and diced Swiss cheese, tossed in a well-flavoured vinaigrette dressing. Garnish with walnut halves and crumbled cooked bacon.

Salade Jardinière

Lettuce leaves (Little Gem), cooked green beans, carrot strips and raw cucumber strips. Vinaigrette dressing. Garnish, if desired, with nasturtiums.

Roman Vegetables

SERVES 4-6

4 small courgettes
2 stalks celery
100g/4oz green beans
4 small carrots, scraped and cut into eighths
12 button mushrooms
12 button onions
½ head cauliflower
1 green pepper, stem, pith and seeds removed

2 red peppers, stems, pith and seeds removed
1 small aubergine
150ml/¼ pint olive oil
2 cloves garlic, quartered
2 bay leaves
Salt and freshly ground pepper
4 tablespoons dry white wine

4 tablespoons wine vinegar
150ml/¼ pint tomato ketchup
2 tablespoons sugar
12 stuffed olives
Lemon juice (optional)
Lettuce leaves and finely chopped parsley, to garnish

1 Cut courgettes into 0.5cm/¼ inch slices. Cut celery, green beans and carrot sticks into 2.5cm/1inch segments. Wash mushrooms and trim stems. Peel onions. Trim cauliflower and break into florets. Cut green and red peppers into thick chunks. Cut unpeeled aubergine into slices 0.5cm/¼ inch thick. Cut each slice into quarters.

2 Heat the olive oil in a large, thick-bottomed casserole. Add vegetables, quartered garlic and bay leaves, and season generously with salt and freshly ground pepper. Cover casserole and simmer vegetables gently over a low heat until the vegetables are tender, but still quite crisp.

3 Combine wine, wine vinegar, tomato ketchup and sugar and stir into casserole. Add stuffed olives and continue to cook gently for another 10 minutes.

4 Remove casserole from the heat and allow vegetables to cool to room temperature. Mix well and chill until ready to serve. Correct seasoning, adding a little lemon juice and a little more salt and freshly ground pepper, if desired.

5 To serve, place crisply cooked vegetables on lettuce leaves and sprinkle with finely chopped parsley.

Artichokes with Walnut Dressing

SERVES 4

4 artichokes
Salt
Juice of ½ lemon
Freshly ground pepper
Finely chopped fresh herbs

Walnut Dressing
150ml/¼ pint double cream
Salt and freshly ground pepper
Walnut oil
Lemon juice

1 Remove the tough outer leaves of artichokes and trim tops of inner leaves. Trim the base and stem of each artichoke with a sharp knife. Cook until tender (30-40 minutes) in a large quantity of boiling salted water, to which you have added the juice of ½ lemon. Artichokes are cooked when a leaf pulls out easily. Turn artichokes upside down to drain.

2 Remove inner leaves of cooked artichokes, leaving a decorative outer ring of 2 or 3 leaves to form a cup around the heart of each artichoke. Season with salt and freshly ground pepper, and chill in the refrigerator.

3 To make walnut dressing: Whip double cream until stiff, flavour with salt and freshly ground pepper, walnut oil and lemon juice to taste.

4 Just before serving, pile artichoke hearts with whipped walnut cream filling and sprinkle with finely chopped herbs.

To Choose and Store Artichokes

Choose artichokes that are fresh and heavy for their size, with supple, tightly closed leaves. Stiff, dry leaves and an 'overblown' appearance generally indicate a tough, woody artichoke.

The size of an artichoke is no indication to its quality, but small ones are better for pickling, medium-sized and large artichokes for serving whole as an appetizer, or in dishes where only the heart is called for.

Artichokes can be stored in the refrigerator, tightly covered, to preserve their moisture.

Japanese Noodles

SERVES 4-6

2 packets Japanese Udon noodles
1 packet dried Chinese mushrooms
2 tablespoons sesame oil
2 tablespoons soy sauce

1 tablespoon vegetable oil
2 tablespoons chopped fresh coriander
* or parsley*

1 Place dried mushrooms in a small bowl and add 900ml/1½ pints boiling water to cover. Let mushrooms steep in water until soft. Squeeze dry. Add 1 tablespoon each sesame oil and soy sauce. Mix well.

2 Bring 900ml/1½ pints water to the boil. Add contents of 2 packets wet Udon noodles to water, together with the contents of small seasoning packets (found in each packet of noodles). Stir until noodles are separated. Cook noodles for 2 minutes.

3 Drain noodles, transfer to a large bowl and add marinated mushrooms and 1 tablespoon each sesame oil, soy sauce and vegetable oil. Stir well and allow noodles to cool.

4 Sprinkle chopped coriander or parsley over the noodles and serve cold as one of a selection of cold hors-d'oeuvres.

Iced Tomato and Roasted Pepper Salad with Watercress

6 large ripe tomatoes
2 roasted red or yellow peppers
1 bunch watercress (sprigs only)
6 tablespoons olive oil
1 tablespoon balsalmic vinegar

1 tablespoon lime juice
2-3 cloves garlic, finely chopped
1 tablespoon fresh oregano or marjoram
Salt and freshly ground pepper
Ice cubes

1 Slice the tomatoes into thin wedges and arrange in a large salad bowl.

2 Core and seed the roasted peppers and cut into segments and add to tomatoes. Top with sprigs of fresh watercress.

3 In a small bowl combine the olive oil, balsalmic vinegar and lime juice. Add the fresh oregano or marjoram, finely chopped garlic and salt and freshly ground pepper to taste.

4 Just before serving, pour the dressing over the salad. Place the ice cubes on top and serve immediately.

Italian Courgette and Bacon Tart

SERVES 6-8

1 23-25cm/9-10-inch fingertip pastry case, baked blind (see page s 214-15)

Filling
½ Spanish onion
100g/4oz bacon
2 tablespoons olive oil
½ chicken stock cube, crumbled

4-6 small courgettes
Salt and freshly ground pepper
4 eggs
300 ml/½ pint double cream
150ml/¼ pint milk
Cayenne pepper
Freshly grated nutmeg
6 tablespoons freshly grated Gruyère cheese

1 Preheat oven to 170°C/325°F/Gas 3.

2 Chop onion finely and sauté in olive oil with crumbled stock cube until onion is soft, stirring constantly so it does not colour. Remove onion from pan with a slotted spoon and reserve.

3 Cut bacon into 0.5cm/¼ inch slices and then cut each slice into 'fingers' about 0.5cm/¼-inch thick. Sauté in olive oil until golden. Remove from pan with slotted spoon and reserve.

4 Wash courgettes and cut off tops and bottoms. Slice courgettes as thinly as you can and sauté slices in remaining fats until lightly coloured. Season to taste with salt and freshly ground pepper. Remove from pan with slotted spoon and reserve.

5 Combine eggs, cream and milk in a mixing bowl and mix thoroughly. Season generously with salt, freshly ground pepper, cayenne pepper and nutmeg.

6 Sprinkle 2 tablespoons grated Gruyère cheese on the bottom of prepared pastry case. Combine sautéed onion, bacon and courgettes and spoon into pastry case, sprinkle with 2 tablespoons grated Gruyère cheese and pour in egg and cream mixture.

7 Sprinkle with remaining Gruyère cheese and bake in a preheated oven (170°C/325°F/Gas 3) for 30-40 minutes or until the custard is set and golden brown.

Prawn and Lobster Quiche

SERVES 6-8

Pastry
225g/8 oz plain flour
1 level tablespoon icing sugar
Generous pinch of salt
125g/5 oz softened butter, diced
1-2 tablespoons iced water

Quiche Filling
150 ml/¼ pint double cream
150 ml/¼ pint milk

150 ml/¼ pint fish stock or canned
  clam juice
4 eggs
¼ small cooked lobster
100g/4 oz small Norwegian prawns
2 tablespoons Cognac
1 tablespoon lemon juice
Salt
Cayenne pepper

1 To make pastry: Sieve flour, sugar and salt into a mixing bowl. Rub in softened butter a little at a time with the tips of the fingers until mixture resembles fine breadcrumbs. Work gently and lightly or mixture will become greasy and heavy. Add just enough iced water to make a good dough. Shape dough lightly into a flattened round, wrap in foil or plastic and put in refrigerator for at least 1 hour to ripen and become firm. If chilled dough is too firm for handling, leave at room temperature until it softens slightly. Then turn out on to a floured board and roll out in usual manner. Place in a 23cm/9 inch pie tin and press out with fingertips.

2 Prick bottom of pastry shell with a fork. Cover with a piece of foil, fill with dried beans and bake 'blind' in a preheated hot oven (230°C/450°F/Gas 8) for 15 minutes. Remove beans and foil. Allow pastry shell to cool.

3 Remove lobster meat from shell and dice. Place diced lobster and prawns in a dish and add Cognac, lemon juice, salt and cayenne pepper to taste.

4 To make quiche filling: Beat cream, milk, fish stock or clam juice and eggs with a whisk. Place diced lobster and prawns on the baked pastry shell. Pour the beaten egg mixture over the lobster and prawns.

5 Bake quiche in the oven (170°C/325°F/Gas 3) for 30 to 40 minutes, or until the custard is set and golden brown.

Pâtés and Terrines

When I was young, pâtés always meant the extremely rich *pâté de foie gras* that we often had as a special occasion feast at Christmas. These expensive pâtés - made in France from livers of specially fattened geese, usually studded with truffles, and eaten with hot, crisp slices of toast and farmhouse butter - were a sensuous treat that the whole family used to look forward to from year to year.

Now that I have been cooking my own pâtés for years, a pâté can mean almost anything that contains a mixture of ground meats, or poultry or game; the mix is 'softened' in flavour with a little ground pork and veal, and then studded with strips of ham, tongue, poultry or game.

One of my favourite pâtés is a delicious green herb pâté, studded for texture and colour contrast with diced tongue, diced ham, diced bacon, and a little diced pork fat and some diced chicken livers sautéed in butter.

I first made *pâté aux herbes* (see page 17) in St Tropez. I had visited a tiny restaurant in upper Provence, and enjoyed a very gutsy herb and ham pâté that I tasted there. Deciding to make it at home, I simmered some fresh leaves of spinach and *blette* in a little butter. I added a little finely chopped pork to the mix, with cream and egg yolks for extra richness. Then the problem was how to recreate the wonderfully herby flavour of the original. It was time to experiment. Did it have thyme in it? Yes, it did have thyme. A little more thyme, a little more rosemary, and a little sage. Now perhaps the flavour was a little *too* rich, so I softened it with a little added cream. Cooking is really like painting . . . all the flavours and aromatics that we use in our daily cooking are like the colours on an artist's palette.

There are two jellied terrines that I like to serve as a refreshing first course for lunches or dinner parties. Cold parsleyed ham (a simpler version of the French classic *Jambon Persillé à la mode de Bourgogne*, and my own more modern and colourful version of salmon and smoked salmon garnished with chopped hard-boiled egg whites and parsley.

The Hedgehog Pâté is a bit of whimsy which forms an appealing 'hedgehog' out of a highly flavoured ham and spice pate covered with aspic and studded with toasted slivered almonds for 'spikes'. This pâté is equally good, of course, served more simply in a terrine or bowl.

Try, too, the Gravad Mackerel recipe on page 18 which used fresh mackerel instead of salmon for an unusual version of the classic Gravad Lax.

Cold Parsleyed Ham

(A simpler version of the French classic
Jambon Persillé de Bourgogne)

SERVES 6-8

900g/2 lb cooked ham (cut in 1 piece)
600ml/1 pint well-flavoured
 chicken stock
150ml/¼ pint dry white wine
Freshly ground pepper

Nutmeg
6-8 tablespoons finely chopped fresh
 parsley, plus enough to dust bowl
2 tablespoons powdered gelatine
1-2 tablespoons tarragon vinegar

1 Cut ham into cubes. Bring chicken stock and wine gently to the boil. Add ham cubes and freshly ground pepper and nutmeg, to taste. (No salt. The ham is salty enough.) Lower heat and simmer very gently for 5 minutes.

2 Drain, reserving stock, and place ham cubes loosely in a wet glass bowl which you have dusted thickly with finely chopped parsley.

3 Soften gelatine in a little water. Stir into stock. Add 6-8 tablespoons parsley and tarragon vinegar. Allow to cool until syrupy, then pour over diced ham. If there is not enough liquid to cover ham, add a little more dry white wine, to cover. Allow to set for 12 hours in the refrigerator before unmoulding.

Cold Parsleyed Salmon

SERVES 6-8

6 27.5cm/11inch strips lightly poached salmon
8 heaped teaspoons powdered gelatine
1 litre/2 pints well-flavoured fish stock

Salt and freshly ground pepper
Diced white of 4 hard-boiled eggs
100-150g/4-6 oz diced smoked salmon
1 bunch parsley, chopped

1 To make aspic: Dissolve gelatine in 8 tablespoons hot water and add to fish stock. Season with salt and freshly ground pepper to taste. Blend in diced egg white, diced smoked salmon and chopped parsley and allow aspic to set until it is syrupy, stirring from time to time.

2 To assemble terrine: Cover bottom of rectangular terrine (29.5 x 8cm/11½ x 3½ inches) with a thin layer of aspic and leave in refrigerator to set. Arrange 2 strips of poached salmon on top of aspic, leaving space between strips. Cover salmon with aspic and return to refrigerator to set . Place another 2 strips of poached salmon on top of aspic, cover with aspic and leave to set. Place remaining 2 strips of fresh salmon on top. Fill terrine with remaining aspic.

3 Place terrine in refrigerator and chill overnight or until set. Serve with cucumber cream (see page 33).

Note : Keep aspic syrupy while aspic-filled terrine sets in refrigerator by immersing bowl containing aspic in a larger bowl of warm water.

Hedgehog Pâté

SERVES 4

550g/1 ¼ lb cooked ham, cut
   into cubes
100g/4oz firm fat from cooked
   ham, cut into cubes
½ Spanish onion, chopped
1 small clove garlic, chopped
2 teaspoons Dijon mustard
1 tablespoon wine vinegar
½ teaspoon anchovy paste
½ teaspoon ground nutmeg

¼ teaspoon each ground
   pepper, ginger, ground cloves
   and dried thyme or oregano
150ml/¼ pint liquid aspic, cooled
   until syrupy
Toasted slivered almonds
2 currants
Small pieces black olive
   for decoration

1 Combine cubed ham and ham fat in bowl of electric blender or food processor and blend until mixture resembles a coarse pâté.

2 Add chopped onion and garlic, Dijon mustard, wine vinegar, anchovy paste, ground nutmeg, ground pepper, ginger, ground cloves and dried thyme or oregano. Blend again until mixture is smooth. Taste and correct seasoning, adding a little more of any of the above aromatics and spices, if necessary.

3 Pack mixture into a large bowl. Cover and refrigerate for 2 days to allow flavours to amalgamate.

4 To form hedgehog: Mould mixture on a flat serving dish and, using a spatula, shape into a smooth oval, bringing the front of hedgehog into a sharp point to represent the 'head'. Brush hedgehog with liquid aspic to give it a translucent look. Stud with toasted slivered almonds for 'spikes', bits of black olive for 'nose', and currants for 'eyes'.

5 Chill in refrigerator until ready to serve. Serve with hot toast and chilled butter.

Pâté aux Herbes

SERVES 8-10

225g/8oz lean pork
4 tablespoons butter
1 Spanish onion, finely chopped
900g/2lb fresh spinach
100g/4oz cooked ham
100g/4oz fresh pork fat
100g/4oz cooked ox tongue
2 cloves garlic, finely chopped
2 tablespoons finely chopped basil
2 tablespoons finely chopped parsley
2 tablespoons finely chopped chervil

24 spikes fresh rosemary, finely chopped
4 eggs, beaten
Salt and freshly ground pepper
Cayenne pepper
Freshly grated nutmeg
150g/6oz chicken livers
150ml/¼ pint double cream
2 tablespoons powdered gelatine
Thin strips of pounded pork fat
Gherkins, for garnish

1 Cut the pork into small cubes. Place in blender or food processor and blend until minced. Melt 2 tablespoons butter in a large frying pan, add onion and sauté, stirring constantly, until transparent. Add spinach and continue to cook, stirring, until spinach has wilted (if fresh). Remove onions and spinach and chop coarsely. Add onion and spinach mixture to pork and blend again. Transfer mixture to a large bowl.

2 Cut ham, pork fat and ox tongue, into 1.5cm/ ⅓ inch cubes and add to green pâté mixture. Then add finely chopped garlic and fresh herbs. (If you use dried herbs, use only half the quantities.)

3 Stir in the beaten eggs and add salt, freshly ground pepper, cayenne pepper and nutmeg to taste.

4 Dice chicken livers and sauté in 2 tablespoons butter until golden.

5 Stir in cream and powdered gelatine (dissolved in a little water) and mix well. Add to pâté mixture and mix again. The raw pâté will now be a loose, spoonable mixture ready for cooking.

6 Line the bottom and sides of an ovenproof terrine with thin strips of pounded pork fat. Spoon pâté mixture into terrine; cover with thin strips of pounded pork fat and cook in the oven (170°C/325°F/Gas 3) for 30 minutes. Lower heat to 150°C/ 300°F/Gas 2 and cook for another 30-40 minutes.

7 Remove from oven to cool, pressing excess juices out of the terrine with a board or the back of a spoon. Serve cold, cut into slices, with gherkins.

Note: to remove pâté from terrine, place terrine in a pan of hot water for a minute or two, then insert a sharp pointed knife all around pâté, loosening it from the sides of the terrine. Turn terrine upside down over serving plate, and the pâté will slide out easily.

Gravad Mackerel

2 even-sized pieces fresh , raw
  mackerel, bone removed
  (about 450g/1 lb each)
8 tablespoons sugar

10 tablespoons salt
1 tablespoon coarsely ground
  pepper
½ teaspoon salt petre
Fresh dill

1 Combine sugar, salt, coarsely ground pepper and salt petre (the latter is not essential, but if obtainable from a chemist should be used to improve colour of dish) and rub mackerel pieces on all sides with this spice mixture.

2 Line the bottom of an earthenware or porcelain terrine or pâté dish with sprigs of fresh dill. Place 1 piece of mackerel on this, skin side down, and sprinkle generously with spice mixture. Add more sprigs fresh dill, then top with second piece of mackerel, skin side up. Place a board cut to fit terrine on top and press down with a weight. Refrigerate for 48 hours.

3 When ready to serve, slice gravad mackerel across the grain into very thin slices and serve as an unusual first course with black bread, unsalted butter and a wedge or two of lemon. The uncooked mackerel will have a fine flavour.

Magic with Stocks and Soups

In the world of good food, nothing offers greater variety for nourishing meals than soup. Fresh-tasting, clear soups are the new fashion in France today, piled high with slivers of chicken and beef and a mosaic of crisp vegetables, or with plump slices of gently poached seafood and a fine *julienne* of crisp vegetables for flavour and colour contrast. I like, too, the great peasant soups of French and Italian country cooking - one-dish dinners made of lentils and pork or game; *haricots blanc*, goose and garlic, or chick peas, chicken and Spanish sausage.

Many of us have our own gardens and through the summer months we can enjoy delicious soups made from home-grown vegetables. The trick is to handle such vegetables almost like seasonings, in a clear meat, poultry or fish-based broth, spiked with a little dry white wine and tomato and given a last-minute pinch of fresh herbs for extra savour; or to purée them with a little well-flavoured stock and double cream and blend them so skilfully that, while you don't taste any one vegetable individually, the result is a triumph of country flavours.

Excellent soups and stocks can also be made quite simply and economically from leftovers. Bones, scraps and carcasses, vegetable tops and leaves, even vegetable peelings and trimmings of meat, poultry or game, can find their way into the soup pot to add flavour and nourishment to a meal.

Basic stocks

Stock - the liquid into which the juice and flavour of various nutritive substances have been drawn by means of long, slow cooking - serves as a foundation for most soups, stews, gravies and sauces.

Stock can be made from various ingredients. Meat and bones, cooked or uncooked, flavoured with vegetables, are the usual basics, but poultry, game or fish combined with vegetables, and even vegetables alone, may all be utilized for this purpose.

Stock (especially meat stock) should be made the day before it is to be used, as best results can be obtained only by long, slow cooking. And it is only when the stock is cold that the fat can be easily skimmed off the surface.

Flavouring the stock

Do not let the flavour of the vegetables overpower the flavour of the meat used in a meat, poultry or game stock; one flavour must not predominate over another. Onions, shallots, carrots, turnips and celery are the vegetables generally used, but leeks, tomatoes, parsnips and mushrooms may also be used for the darker stocks.

Vegetables are usually diced or left whole for stocks. They must not be allowed to cook too long in the stock, for after a certain time they tend to absorb flavours instead of adding to them. If a large quantity of meat is used and the stock is likely to cook for many hours, the vegetables should not be put in at the beginning of the cooking time, or they should be lifted out before the stock has finished cooking. Stock vegetables may be served as a separate vegetable dish on their own, or made into a vegetable purée, with a little butter and cream added.

Different kinds of stock

Brown stock: Beef, beef bones and vegetables with sometimes a little veal or some chicken or game bones added for extra flavour.
White stock: White meat such as veal, rabbit, chicken or mutton, and vegetables with sometimes a calf's foot added for extra flavour.
Fish stock: Fish or fish trimmings with vegetables and sometimes shellfish trimmings added for extra flavour.
Game stock: Game or game bones and trimmings and vegetables
Vegetable stock:This is made from vegetables alone, either dried or fresh or a mixture of the two. For vegetarian soups and dishes.
Glaze:A stock which is so much reduced in quantity that it forms an almost solid substance when cold. It is a means of preserving any surplus stock.

Different kinds of soups

Clear soups or consommés are made from stocks as above, but clarified by adding beaten egg white and crushed egg shells to the stock and bringing it to the boil. The impurities in the soup adhere to the egg white and shell mass and can then be strained out through a fine muslin.

Broths differ from clear soups in that they are unclarified. The meat or poultry or game with which they are made is served either in the soup or after it as a separate course. A broth is usually garnished with rice or barley and diced vegetables

Thickened soups can be made of fish, meat or vegetables. They generally have some stock as their basis. The soups are thickened with flour, arrowroot, cornflour, tapioca or sago. In some of the richer soups, a combination of eggs and cream is used.

Pureés are perhaps the simplest and most economical kind of soup. They can be made of almost any vegetable, either fresh or dried, and of meat, game and fish. They sometimes have farinaceous substances such as rice, barley or macaroni added. A small amount of diced butter is often added at the very last moment.

Rich Beef Stock

MAKES 1.5 LITRES/ 3 PINTS

1.4kg/3 lb shin or neck of beef on the bone (see Step 1)
450g/1 lb shin of veal on the bone (see Step 1)
1 small ham bone (about 225g/ 8oz) or 100g/4oz lean ham
2 Spanish onions, roughly chopped
3 large carrots, roughly chopped
2 leeks, thickly sliced
3-4 stalks celery, thickly sliced

50g/2 oz beef dripping
A few mushroom stalks or trimmings
2-3 soft over-ripe tomatoes
Salt
3 sprigs parsley
1 sprig thyme or a pinch of dried thyme
1 bay leaf
1 clove
9 peppercorns

1 Ask a butcher to remove the meat from the shin (or neck) of beef and shin of veal, and to chop the bones up into large chunks.

2 Preheat oven to very hot (240°C/475°F/Gas 9).

3 Trim any excess fat from the meat.

4 Put beef and veal bones, and ham bone, if available, in a roasting tin. Add roughly chopped onions and carrots and thickly sliced leeks and celery, and dot with dripping.

5 Roast bones and vegetables in the oven for 40-45 minutes, turning occasionally, until richly browned.

6 Scrape contents of roasting tin into large saucepan, casserole or stockpot. Add boned meat, ham (if used), mushroom stalks or trimmings and soft tomatoes.

7 Add 300ml/½ pint cold water to roasting tin and bring to the boil, scraping bottom and sides of tin with a wooden spoon to dislodge all crusty bits and sediment. Pour over vegetables, then add 3 litres/6 pints cold water.

8 Place pan over a low heat and bring to the boil. Allow scum to settle on the surface, then skim off with a slotted spoon. Add a little salt (not too much - remember stock will reduce), to draw out more scum. Skim again.

9 When all the scum has been drawn out of the meat and bones, throw in herbs, bay leaf, clove and peppercorns, and leave stock to simmer gently for 3 hours.

10 Strain stock through a fine sieve into a large bowl and allow to cool before skimming off fat. Store until ready to be used.

Note: Meat can be eaten with coarse salt and freshly ground pepper, or combined with fresh vegetables to make another, less rich, portion of stock.

Rich Chicken Stock

MAKES 1.5 LITRES/ 3 PINTS

1 fine, fat boiling fowl (about 1.8-2.2kg/4-5 lb complete)
1 large veal knuckle
Salt
6-8 peppercorns
2 leeks, sliced
3 large carrots, sliced
1 Spanish onion, sliced

2 tomatoes, seeded and sliced
4 stalks celery, sliced
1 bouquet garni (2 sprigs parsley, 2 sprigs thyme and 1 bay leaf)
1 clove garlic, mashed with the flat of a knife
1 chicken stock cube

1 Put the fowl in a large stockpot, add the veal knuckle (for its extra gelatine content) and cover with 3 litres/6 pints cold water. Add salt to taste, and peppercorns, and bring slowly to the boil. Skim any impurities from the top of the liquid, then reduce the heat and simmer, with the liquid barely bubbling, for at least 1 hour. The stock will begin to get cloudy as the essences are released from the chicken. As these bubble gently to the surface, skim them off to remove all impurities from the stock. This simple skimming stage is one of the most important parts of soup-making and makes all the difference between a clear stock and a cloudy one.

2 Add sliced leeks, carrots, onion, tomatoes, celery, bouquet garni, garlic and chicken stock cube, and continue to simmer very gently for 1½-2 hours longer, or until the chicken is cooked through.

3 Remove fat, correct seasoning and strain the stock through a fine sieve, or a piece of muslin in a colander. Cool stock and store in the refrigerator for further use.

Glace de Viande

3.6kg/8 lb beef and veal bones
1 large Spanish onion, cut in half
1-2 chicken carcasses
225g/8oz carrots, cut in 5cm/
  2 inch segments
225g/8oz celery stalks and leaves,
  cut in 5 cm/2 inch segments

450g/1 lb onions, cut in quarters
6-8 level tablespoons beef dripping
450ml/¾ pint canned peeled
  tomatoes

Note: Use half quantities of the above if
you do not possess a very large stockpot.

1 Ask a butcher to supply you with 3.6kg/8 lb beef and veal bones, with some meat on them, chopped into 10-12.5cm/4-5 inch segments. You'll have to give him warning.

2 Sear cut sides of onion in a griddle pan, or a large thick-bottomed frying pan, using no fat. The onion should be very dark on the cut surface.

3 Brown the bones, together with 1 or 2 chicken carcasses, carrots, celery and onions, in beef dripping.

4 When bones and vegetables are well browned, transfer them to a very large stockpot or a deep casserole. Fill the pot with unsalted water; add browned onion halves and peeled tomatoes and simmer bones and vegetables in the lowest of ovens overnight.

5 Strain out the bones and vegetables. Return stock to a clean stockpot and cook until reduced to half or less of the original quantity, skimming off fat and impurities as they rise to the surface.

6 Strain reduced stock through a muslin-lined sieve into a clean saucepan and cook again, stirring frequently, until very thick. Pour into small jars, cool, and store in the refrigerator until ready to use.

This professional kitchen recipe for *glace de viande* produces a concentrated jelly of rubbery consistency that keeps for months in the refrigerator. Make *glace de viande* for yourself and for your friends. Tell them to use a teaspoon or two to add fabulous flavour to the pan juices of pan-fried steaks and chops, to butter or oil before you toss pasta or vegetables and add more of this delicious mixture to strengthen consommés and soups and add flavour to casseroles and sauces. It is a magic ingredient.

Cream of Spinach Soup

SERVES 6

900g/2lb fresh spinach or 450g/
  1lb frozen chopped spinach
4 tablespoons butter
300ml/½ pint double cream
300-450ml/½–¾ pint chicken stock

(see page 22)
Juice of ½ lemon
Salt and freshly ground pepper
1 finely chopped hard-boiled egg

1 If using fresh spinach, wash leaves in several changes of cold water, nipping off any tough stems and discarding yellowed leaves. Drain well in a colander, pressing out excess moisture, and chop roughly.

2 Melt butter in a heavy saucepan and add spinach (fresh or in frozen block). Simmer gently, stirring occasionally, for 8-10 minutes, or until spinach is soft.

3 Purée spinach in an electric blender. Pour back into rinsed out pan.

4 Stir in cream and dilute to taste with chicken stock, using 300ml/½ pint if you want a very thick, rich soup; 450ml/¾ pint for a lighter consistency. Heat through over a moderate heat, stirring.

5 Season to taste with a little lemon juice and salt and freshly ground pepper. Serve hot, each portion garnished with a sprinkling of chopped hard-boiled egg.

Vichyssoise

SERVES 4-6

6 large leeks
4 tablespoons butter
4 medium potatoes
900ml/1 ½ pints chicken stock
  (see page 22)

Salt and freshly ground pepper
Finely grated nutmeg
300ml/½ pint double cream
Finely chopped chives

1 Cut the green tops from the leeks and cut the white parts into 2.5cm/1inch lengths.

2 Sauté the white parts gently in butter until soft. Do not allow to brown.

3 Peel and slice potatoes; add to leeks, with chicken stock, salt and freshly ground pepper and finely grated nutmeg to taste, and simmer until vegetables are cooked.

4 Force vegetables and stock through a fine sieve, or blend in an electric blender until smooth. Chill.

5 Just before serving, add cream and serve sprinkled with chives.

Green Consommé

SERVES 6-8

1.5 litres/3 pints well-flavoured
  beef stock (see page 21)
1 ripe avocado pear
Lemon juice

6 tablespoons diced cooked green beans
6 tablespoons frozen peas
Salt and white pepper
Tabasco

1 Peel, stone and dice avocado pear. Strain lemon juice over avocado and toss well to preserve colour.

2 Add diced cooked green beans and frozen peas to avocado. Flavour vegetables with salt and white pepper and toss again so that flavours permeate vegetables.

3 Bring beef stock gently to the boil. Skim, if necessary, and season with a drop or two of Tabasco.

4 When ready to serve, add prepared vegetables and return soup to the boil.

Gazpacho - Iced Spanish Soup

According to Brillat-Savarin, a woman who can't make soup should not be allowed to marry. The Spanish solved this ticklish problem early in their history with a chilled summer soup that requires absolutely no cooking.

To make *gazpacho*: blend 6 tomatoes and 1 garlic clove in electric blender. Add 1 to 2 tablespoons juice from a finely grated onion, and ½ cucumber, peeled, seeded and cut into cubes, and blend again. Strain into a large tureen or serving bowl and chill.

Just before serving, blend 6 tablespoons olive oil, 4 tablespoons lemon juice and 450ml/¾ pint chilled tomato juice. Add to puréed vegetables, mix well and season with salt and cayenne pepper to taste.

Serve *gazpacho* with individual bowls of raw vegetables (diced tomatoes, onion, cucumber and green pepper) and fried garlic-flavoured *croûtons*. Guests help themselves to a little of each.

Try the basic recipe for *gazpacho* , then ring the changes by stirring in 2-4 tablespoons of fresh breadcrumbs, or a little well-flavoured mayonnaise, finely ground almonds or the beaten yolk of an egg. Or add a little gelatine and serve it slightly jellied.

Summer Tomato Soup

SERVES 4-6

1.25kg/2½ lb ripe tomatoes	*300ml/½ pint double cream, chilled*
Juice and finely grated rind of 1 lemon	*225g/8oz ham, cut into 0.5 cm/¼ inch dice*
4 level teaspoons castor sugar	*225g/8oz cucumber, peeled, seeded and cut into 0.5cm/¼ inch dice*
1-1½ level tablespoons grated onion	*4 level tablespoons chopped chives*
Salt and crushed dried chillies	

1 Quarter tomatoes and blend to a purée in an electric blender. Put purée through a fine sieve.

2 Stir in lemon juice and rind, sugar, grated onion and salt and crushed dried chillies, to taste. Chill.

3 Just before serving, add chilled double cream and mix well. Pour into a bowl and garnish with diced ham, cucumber and finely chopped chives.

New Ways with Sauces

In French cooking, the word sauce means any liquid or semi-liquid that complements a dish - the lightly thickened gravy that accompanies the Sunday roast; the cream sauce for a steamed cauliflower; the melted butter and lemon dressing for a grilled or poached fish; and salad dressings, from a simple vinaigrette sauce to a mustard and lemon-flavoured mayonnaise.

In other words, sauces - no matter how simple - are important in cooking. But don't make the mistake of thinking that sauces should be thick and rich. Chefs today use as little flour in cooking as possible - to make the sauce more delicate in flavour, more suave in texture and more easily assimilated by the digestive system.

The heart of every sauce is a flavoursome stock, made by reducing home-made meat, poultry or fish broth to a concentrated essence. This liquid ingredient - whether home-made beef, veal, fish or poultry stock, or simply milk or cream - is most important to the final quality and flavour of your sauce.

In French cooking terminology, reduction is a magic word. Magic only because this terribly simple process (it just means cooking stocks over a high heat to reduce them to a third or a quarter of their original quantity before adding them to the sauce) gives such intensity of flavour to the finished sauce.

It is no secret that French chefs use more liquid in their sauces (almost twice as much) as do most other cooks. Consequently, they cook them longer, and this concentration and blending of flavours makes their sauces more suave, more transparent, and more delicious.

The secret of easy sauce-making, therefore, is the careful reduction of your sauce by slow simmering over a low heat, leaving the sauce thicker in consistency, smoother in texture and more concentrated in flavour.

To strain sauce

Always strain all sauces before serving, except of course, those which have chopped ingredients in them. A conical strainer (making it easier to direct the flow of liquid) is best. For a finer sauce, line the strainer with a clean cloth to give a smooth, glossy appearance.

To add butter to a sauce

French chefs often incorporate finely diced butter into a sauce just before serving. The butter is usually whisked into the strained sauce with a wire whisk after the sauce has been taken off the heat. This makes the sauce thicker and more flavoursome. Do not return the sauce to the heat after you have whisked in the butter or it will separate and become fatty.

To keep sauce warm

When a sauce has to stand for some time before serving, place the pan of sauce into a larger saucepan containing hot (not boiling) water, or in a bain-marie. Cover the saucepan to prevent a skin forming. With thicker sauces, a spoonful of liquid (water, stock or milk) or melted butter may be run over the top. Just before serving, whisk this protective covering into the sauce.

White sauces

Are you frightened of making sauces? Many of my friends tell me they are, and I don't really know why, for making a classic French sauce is very easy. Sauce Béchamel, for instance, the classic white sauce of French cooking, goes way back in culinary history to the time of Louis XIV of France. Its creation is credited to the Marquis de Béchamel, the king's Maitre d'Hôtel, who ran the royal palace at Versailles - at any rate, it was named after him because he was a famous gourmet. Cooks of the time were apt to name their dishes after their patron whether or not he actually created it.

In the days of the Marquis de Béchamel, the sauce was more complicated than it is now. The original Sauce Béchamel combined a partridge, ham, chicken and perhaps a guinea fowl to flavour the rich, creamy sauce we know today.

Variations on the Béchamel theme

Add a touch of mustard and a tablespoon of capers and you have a mustard and caper sauce. Then add a little finely chopped fresh herbs and you have a terrific sauce for eggs, fish and even poached lamb.

Stir a little tomato purée (fresh or canned) into the basic sauce to give it a pale blush, flavour it with a little Madeira or brandy and add a touch of cream to make it just that much richer. This makes a very subtle sauce for poached fish, boiled eggs and steamed vegetables.

Or, for a more exotic variation, add a little lobster butter to the above sauce. Lobster butter is easily prepared from cooked lobster shells, pounded in a mortar and them simmered in 100g/4oz butter with a bay leaf, a ½ onion, a little bit of garlic, some tomato purée and some brandy. Chill the sauce in the refrigerator, then just skim off the top of your juices and you have lobster butter. So don't throw away those lobster shells. Keep them in the fridge to give a wonderfully buttery richness to your sauces for poached fish.

Professional cooks use a spoonful of *glace de viande* (see page 23) to swirl into the pan juices of cooked meats to create a deliciously limpid sauce in a twinkling. This cook's aid keeps indefinitely in a stoppered jar in the refrigerator, and is well worth the trouble and expense involved. Use only a teaspoon or two with an equal quantity of lemon juice to create a delicious sauce from the pan juices of grilled or pan-fried steaks, chops, liver or kidneys. I like, too, to whisk a bit into melted butter with almonds or pine nuts before tossing this simple sauce with cooked noodles or rice as an accompaniment to meat, fish or poultry. And it is an invaluable 'strengthener' for beef and game soups and consommés.

Butter always contains a little milk which, when brought to a high heat, can make a sauce 'gritty' or slightly discoloured. To solve this problem I usually clarify butter before using it for a delicate sauce by melting it in a small, thick-bottomed, enamelled saucepan over a very low heat. The butter foams, and the foam falls gently to the bottom of the saucepan, leaving the clarified butter as clear as oil. Be careful when you decant this transparent liquid not to disturb any of the white sediment at the bottom. Use as directed.

Basic Sauce Béchamel

4-5 tablespoons butter
½ onion, minced
2 tablespoons flour
600ml/1 pint hot milk or whipping cream
2 tablespoons lean veal or ham, finely chopped

1 small sprig thyme
½ bay leaf
White peppercorns
Freshly grated nutmeg

1 In a thick-bottomed saucepan, or in the top of a double saucepan, melt 2 tablespoons butter and cook onion in it over a low heat until transparent. Stir in flour and cook for a few minutes, stirring constantly, until mixture cooks through but does not take on colour.

2 Add hot milk or cream and cook, stirring constantly, until mixture is thick and smooth.

3 In another saucepan, simmer finely chopped lean veal or ham in 1 tablespoon butter over a very low heat. Season with thyme, bay leaf, white peppercorns and grated nutmeg. Cook for 5 minutes, stirring to keep veal or ham from over-browning.

4 Add meat to the sauce and cook over hot water for 45 minutes to 1 hour, stirring occasionally. When reduced to two-thirds of the original quantity, strain sauce through a fine sieve into a bowl, pressing meat and onion well to extract all the liquid. Cover surface of sauce with tiny pieces of butter to keep film from forming. When ready to serve, beat butter coating into the sauce and warm through.

Mornay Sauce

5-6 tablespoons butter
½ onion, minced
2 tablespoons flour
600ml/1 pint hot milk
2 tablespoons lean veal or
  ham, finely chopped
1 small sprig thyme

½ bay leaf
White peppercorns
Freshly grated nutmeg
2 egg yolks, slightly beaten
Cream
2-3 tablespoons grated
  cheese (Parmesan cheese or Swiss cheese)

1 In a thick-bottomed saucepan, or the top of a double saucepan, melt 2 tablespoons butter and cook onion in it over a low heat until transparent. Stir in flour and cook for a few minutes, stirring constantly, until mixture cooks through but does not take on colour.

2 Add hot milk and cook, stirring constantly, until mixture is thick and smooth.

3 In another saucepan, simmer lean veal or ham in 1 tablespoon butter over a very low heat. Season with thyme, bay leaf, white peppercorns and grated nutmeg. Cook for 5 minutes, stirring to keep veal or ham from over-browning.

4 Add veal or ham to the sauce and cook over hot water for 45 minutes to 1 hour, stirring occasionally. When reduced to two-thirds of the original quantity strain sauce through a fine sieve into a bowl, pressing meat and onion well to extract all the liquid.

5 Mix slightly beaten egg yolks with a little cream and combine with sauce. Cook, stirring constantly, until it just reaches boiling point. Add 2-3 tablespoons butter and grated cheese. Cover surface of sauce with tiny pieces of butter to keep film from forming.

Basic Sauce Espagnole

2 tablespoons butter
1 small onion, thinly sliced
2 tablespoons flour
750ml/1 ¼ pints well-flavoured
brown stock
1 small carrot, sliced
1 small turnip, sliced
1 stalk celery, sliced or ¼
teaspoon celery seed

4 mushrooms, sliced
2-4 tomatoes or 1-2 tablespoons
tomato purée
1 bouquet garni (3 sprigs parsley,
1 sprig thyme and 1 bay leaf)
2 cloves
12 black peppercorns
Salt and crushed dried chillies

1 Heat butter in a thick-bottomed saucepan until it browns. Add onion and simmer, stirring, until golden. Stir in flour and cook, stirring constantly, for a minute or two longer. The good colour of your sauce depends upon the thorough browning of these ingredients without allowing them to burn.

2 Remove saucepan from the heat and pour in the stock. Return to heat and stir until it comes to the boil. Allow to boil for 5 minutes, skimming all scum from the top with a perforated spoon.

3 Add carrot, turnip, celery, mushrooms and tomatoes or tomato purée to the stock, with the bouquet garni, cloves, peppercorns, and salt and crushed dried chillies, to taste. Simmer the sauce gently for at least ½ hour, stirring occasionally and skimming when necessary. Strain through a fine sieve. Remove fat. Reheat before serving.

Madeira Sauce

600ml/1 pint sauce espagnole
(see above)
6 tablespoons Madeira

1 Reduce sauce espagnole to half the original quantity.

2 Add Madeira. Heat the sauce well, but do not let it boil, or the flavour of the wine will be lost.

Sauce Hollandaise

1 teaspoon lemon juice
Salt and white pepper
100g/4oz softened butter

4 egg yolks
Lemon juice

1 Combine lemon juice, 1 tablespoon cold water, and salt and white pepper in the top of a double saucepan or bain-marie.

2 Divide butter into four equal pieces.

3 Add the egg yolks and a quarter of the butter to the liquid in the saucepan, and stir the mixture rapidly and constantly with a wire whisk over hot (not boiling) water until the butter is melted and the mixture begins to thicken. Add the second piece of butter and continue whisking. As the mixture thickens and the second piece of butter melts, add the third piece of butter, stirring from the bottom of the pan until it is melted. Be careful not to allow the water over which the sauce is cooking to boil at any time. Add rest of butter, beating until it melts and is incorporated in the sauce.

4 Remove top part of saucepan from heat and continue to beat for 2-3 minutes. Replace saucepan over hot (not boiling) water for 2 minutes more, beating constantly until you have a rich, creamy emulsion. 'Finish' sauce with a few drops of lemon juice. Strain and serve.

Cucumber Cream

150ml/¼ pint double
cream, whipped
Salt

Lemon juice
½ cucumber, peeled, seeded and diced
Crushed dried chillies

1 Flavour whipped cream with salt and lemon juice to taste.

2 Fold diced cucumber into the cream. Season with crushed dried chillies and chill until ready to use.

Sauces

Mayonnaise

2 egg yolks
Salt and freshly ground pepper
½ teaspoon Dijon mustard

Lemon juice
300ml/½ pint olive oil

1 Place egg yolks (make sure gelatinous thread of the egg is removed), salt, freshly ground pepper and mustard in a bowl. Twist a cloth wrung out in very cold water round the bottom of the bowl to keep it steady and cool. Using a wire whisk, fork or wooden spoon, beat the seasoned egg yolks to a smooth paste.

2 Add a little lemon juice (the acid helps the emulsion), and beat in about a quarter of the olive oil, drop by drop. Add a little more lemon juice to the mixture and then, a little more quickly now, add more olive oil, beating all the while. Continue adding olive oil and beating until the sauce has a good thick consistency. Correct seasoning (more salt, freshly ground pepper and lemon juice) as desired. If you are making the mayonnaise a day before use, stir in 1 tablespoon boiling water when it reaches the desired consistency. This will keep it from turning or separating.

Notes: If the mayonnaise should curdle, break another egg yolk into a clean bowl and gradually beat the curdled mayonnaise in. Your mayonnaise will begin to 'take' immediately.

If mayonnaise is to be used for a salad, thin it down considerably with dry white wine, vinegar or lemon juice. If it is to be used for coating meat, poultry or fish, add a little liquid aspic to stiffen it.

If sauce is to be kept for several hours before serving, cover the bowl with a cloth wrung out in very cold water to prevent a skin forming.

Egg Dishes, Omelettes and Soufflés

The greatest virtue of the egg is that it is always there, handy in the refrigerator, ready to lend its sophisticated magic to delicate little ramekins of eggs and cream, light and insubstantial soufflés and moistly golden omelettes whenever there are unexpected guests.

We depend on the egg - one of the great basics of all cookery - to enrich and flavour chicken soups and sauces; to bind croquettes, meat loaves, and stuffings for meat, poultry and game; to coat meat, fish and vegetables for deep-frying; to add substance to batters and richness to cakes and pastry, and to act as the foundation for sauces made from butter and oil - mayonnaise and sauce Hollandaise (see pages 33 and 34). I like to use raw eggs to dress a salad, and to add colour and quality to a spaghetti sauce. Even the shell can be used to clarify consommés and jellies.

Soft-Boiled Eggs Perfect soft boiled eggs are easy once you know how: just slip the eggs (they must be at room temperature; if you use them straight from the refrigerator, the shells will crack) gently with a spoon, one by one, into a saucepan with just enough boiling water to cover them. If only half the egg is immersed in the water, it will not cook evenly. Lower the heat until water is just barely bubbling and allow 3 minutes for a classic soft-boiled egg – the white coagulated but still on the soft side and the golden yolk runny – or ½ to 1 minute more if it is to be set pretty firm.

Hard-Boiled Eggs Put the required number of eggs (at room temperature as above) into a saucepan of boiling water, lowering them in carefully with a slotted spoon to avoid breaking the shells. Allow the water to come to a boil again and then cook the eggs for exactly 10 minutes. Lift eggs out and plunge them at once into cold water. They will shell more easily.

Oeufs sur le Plat

SERVES 4

8 eggs
2 tablespoons butter

Salt and freshly ground pepper
Cayenne pepper

1 Lightly butter 4 flat heatproof dishes and break the eggs into them without breaking the yolks. Season with salt and freshly ground pepper and a pinch of cayenne, and place the remaining butter in small pieces on the top.

2 Bake in a preheated oven (170°C/325°F/Mark 3) for 4-5 minutes, or until the whites are set but not hard. Serve hot in the dishes in which the eggs were cooked.

Eggs Lucullus – for Special Occasions

SERVES 4

4 hard-boiled eggs
4 small lettuce leaves
8 tomato wedges
8 tablespoons well-flavoured

mayonnaise (see page 34)
4 tablespoons sour cream
2-3 teaspoons black caviare*, or, for
simpler occasions, red caviare*

1 Shell eggs. Cut each egg in half lengthways and arrange 2 half eggs per plate, cut side down, on individual salad plates. Garnish each serving with a small lettuce leaf and 2 tomato wedges.

2 Blend mayonnaise with sour cream and mask each half-egg completely with a tablespoon of mayonnaise, tapping the bottom of the dish if the mayonnaise does not flow smoothly over the egg of its own accord.

3 Dot top of each egg with a few grains of caviare and chill lightly until ready to serve.

* This recipe is really only effective when *real* black caviare is used – a half teaspoon of either Beluga or Sevruga for special occasions, or a little more of the red caviare (salmon roe) for a less expensive version. Lumpfish roe, though colourful, does not have the same savour.

Baked Eggs with Cream

SERVES 4

150ml/¼ pint double cream
2 tablespoons grated
  Gruyère cheese
2 tablespoons lemon juice
2 tablespoons dry white wine

1-2 teaspoons prepared mustard
Salt and freshly ground pepper
8 eggs
Butter
Buttered breadcrumbs

1 Mix together double cream, grated cheese, lemon juice and wine. Add mustard, and salt and freshly ground pepper to taste.

2 Break eggs into individual buttered ramekins or casseroles, 2 eggs in each.

3 Cover the eggs with the sauce and sprinkle buttered breadcrumbs over each ramekin. Place ramekins in a pan of hot water, bring the water surrounding the ramekins to the boil again and bake in a preheated oven (190°C/375°F/Gas 5) for about 15 minutes.

Scrambled Eggs Provençal

SERVES 6

9 eggs
Salt and freshly ground
  pepper
Cayenne pepper
6 slices white bread
Butter

Olive oil
12 anchovy fillets, sliced in
  half lengthways
Black olives
3 tablespoons finely
  chopped parsley

1 Break the eggs into a mixing bowl and add salt, freshly ground pepper, and cayenne pepper to taste. Mix lightly with a fork.

2 Cut white bread into rounds about 10cm/4 inches in diameter and sauté lightly in a little butter and olive oil until just golden. Keep warm.

3 Scramble the eggs in butter and olive oil until they are just soft (not too firm).

4 Spoon the scrambled eggs on to the bread rounds and garnish with a latticework of thin anchovy strips. Fill each lattice with a halved black olive and sprinkle with finely chopped parsley.

Oeufs Mollets Florentine

4 eggs
Salt
4 rounds of hot buttered toast

Florentine sauce
75g/ 3oz spinach leaves
25g/ 10z watercress leaves

½ pint well-flavoured hollandaise sauce
  (see below)
1 tablespoon each finely chopped
  spinach, watercress, flat leafed parsley
  and tarragon
1 tablespoon lemon juice
Freshly ground pepper

1 Wash spinach leaves, discarding any yellow leaves. Trim stalks. Wash sprigs of watercress.

2 Plunge prepared watercress and spinach into a small pan of boiling salted water. Bring back to the boil and simmer for 5 minutes. Drain well and press dry between the folds of a clean kitchen towel or absorbent paper.

3 Pound blanched spinach and watercress to a paste in a mortar (or purée in an electric blender). Add to hollandaise sauce and mix well.

4 Stir finely-chopped spinach, watercress, flat-leafed parsley tarragon and lemon juice into the sauce and season with salt and freshly ground pepper, to taste.

To make hollandaise sauce:
In the top of a double saucepan or bain-marie, combine 1 teaspoon lemon juice with 1 teaspoon cold water and a pinch each of salt and white pepper. Put 225g/ 8oz softened butter on a plate and divide into 4 pieces of equal size. Add 4 egg yolks and 1 piece of butter to the liquid in the pan and place over hot, but not boiling, water. Stir rapidly with a wire whisk for about 5 minutes, or until the butter has melted completely and the mixture begins to thicken, making sure the water underneath never comes to the boil. Incorporate the remaining pieces of butter, one at a time, into the sauce, whisking vigorously and stirring form the bottom of the pan as you do so. When the sauce is thick and emulsified, beat for 2-3 minutes longer. Then correct seasoning, adding more salt, white pepper or lemon juice to taste. Strain, if necessary and use as above.

Oeufs Mollets Florentine

Omelette Ratatouille

SERVES 2-3 GENEROUSLY

8 tablespoons olive oil
1 Spanish onion, sliced
1 green pepper, diced
1 aubergine, diced
2 small courgettes, cut in thin slices
2-4 ripe tomatoes, peeled,
  seeded and chopped

Salt and freshly ground pepper
1 tablespoon chopped parsley
Pinch of marjoram or oregano
Pinch of basil
1 clove garlic, crushed
8 eggs
1-2 tablespoons melted butter

1 Heat half the olive oil in a heatproof casserole. Add onion slices and sauté until transparent. Add diced green pepper and aubergine and cook for 5 minutes. Add courgettes and tomatoes. Cover pan and simmer the vegetables gently (do not fry) for about 30 minutes.

2 Add salt and freshly ground pepper to taste, parsley, marjoram or oregano, basil and crushed garlic. Cook uncovered for about 10-15 minutes, or until the ratatouille ingredients are crisp-tender.

3 Beat eggs lightly with a fork. Season to taste with salt and freshly ground pepper.

4 Heat remaining oil in a large omelette pan. Pour in eggs and stir over a moderate heat until they begin to thicken and have set underneath.

5 Spoon ratatouille mixture down centre, reserving 2 or 3 tablespoons for garnish.

6 Continue to cook omelette until firm and golden brown on the underside but still creamy on top. Slide it up one side of the pan and fold it over on itself.

7 Slip folded omelette out carefully on to a heated serving dish. Brush with melted butter and garnish with remaining ratatouille mixture. Serve immediately.

Spanish Tortilla with Uncooked Tomato Sauce

SERVES 4-6

Olive oil
2 potatoes, peeled and diced
½ large Spanish onion,
  coarsely chopped
½ green or red pepper, coarsely
  chopped
Salt and freshly ground pepper
6-8 eggs, well beaten

Tomato Sauce:
700g/ 1lb 8oz ripe tomatoes, peeled
seeded and chopped
1 clove garlic, finely chopped
Extra-virgin olive oil
Lemon juice
Salt and freshly ground pepper

1 Heat 2 tablespoons olive oil in a medium-sized frying pan. Add potatoes, onion and pepper and cook, stirring constantly, until vegetables are soft. Season generously with salt and freshly ground pepper. Keep warm.

2 Season well-beaten eggs to taste with salt and freshly ground pepper. Heat 2 tablespoons olive oil in a large frying pan. Pour beaten eggs into the pan, lifting up edges of the eggs with a spatula to allow uncooked egg to run under. Add sautéed vegetables, and continue to cook, lifting up tortilla with a spatula, until omelette has a golden crust on the bottom. Then place a large plate on the omelette pan and invert plate so that the omelette is on the plate, crust side up.

3 Scrape free any crusty bits from pan and add a little more olive oil. Return omelette to pan, moist side down, and continue to cook until it has browned on both sides. Cut in wedges and serve.

4 *To make the uncooked tomato sauce:*
In a medium sized bowl, combine the peeled, seeded and diced tomatoes and finely chopped garlic. Add judt enough virgin olive oil to just cover the tomatoes. Season with lemon juice and salt and freshly ground pepper, to taste. Mix well and place bowl in the refrigerator for at least 2 hours to allow flavours to blend before serving.

Mixed Vegetable Frittata

SERVES 6-8

6 eggs
2 egg whites, beaten
½ Spanish onion
Olive oil
Butter
½ vegetable stock cube
2 tablespoons each of finely
  chopped flat leafed parsley,
  coriander and basil

Vegetable filling
½ packet French beans, topped
  and tailed
½ packet baby asparagus spears
2 small courgettes, cut into strips
1 small aubergine, cut into strips
½ red pepper, cut into strips
Salt and crushed dried chillies

Garnish:
Sprigs of fresh herbs
Small yellow and red cherry tomatoes

1 To prepare vegetables: In a small saucepan, blanch vegetables of your choice, using all the vegetables listed for the vegetable filling or just one, or more, according to availability; cover vegetables in just enough cold water to cover them. Bring to the boil. Boil for 1-2 minutes and then drain. If using several vegetables, blanch them separately. Season vegetables with salt and crushed dried chillies.

2 To prepare eggs: In a small frying pan, sauté diced onion in 2 tablespoons olive oil and 1 tablespoon butter with ½ vegetable stock cube until onion is transparent. In a large bowl beat eggs, fold in beaten egg whites and add sautéd onions and fresh herbs and mix well. Reserve.

3 To cook vegetables: In a large frying-pan, heat 2 tablespoons olive oil and 2 tablespoons butter. When fat begins to sizzle, pour onion, herb and egg mixture into pan; sprinkle well-seasoned blanched vegetables over egg mixture and cook over a medium heat (adding a little more butter or oil to the pan if necessary) for 4-5 minutes.

4 Place a large round serving dish (larger than the frying pan) over the frittata and turn it over on the plate. Then slide the frittata back into the pan to cook for a few more minutes, or until it is golden brown on both sides.

5 To serve: slide the frittata out on to a heated serving dish and garnish dish with sprigs of fresh herbs and small yellow and red cherry tomatoes. I often serve this delicious dish with a chilled uncooked tomato sauce (see page 43).

Mixed Vegetable Frittata

French Flat Omelette

SERVES 3-4

Butter
175g/6oz smoked bacon (in one
  piece if possible) cut in small dice
1½ Spanish onions, thinly sliced
Salt and freshly ground pepper
8 eggs

3 tablespoons olive oil
2-3 tablespoons finely chopped basil
Sprigs of fresh watercress
Quartered tomatoes

1 Melt 50g/2oz butter in a large saucepan and saute the diced bacon and sliced onions until the onions are soft and golden. Season generously with salt and freshly ground pepper. Remove the pan from the heat.

2 Break the eggs into a bowl. Stir vigorously with a fork or wire whisk until the yolks and whites are just mixed adding 25g/1oz butter in small pieces. Season lightly with salt and freshly ground pepper.

3 Heat a large, heavy-based frying pan over a moderate heat. Add 2 tablespoons olive oil, then pour in the egg mixture and cook the omelette, lifting the edges to permit the liquid egg to run underneath and shaking the pan to prevent sticking. When the egg begins to set, sprinkle with chopped basil, bacon and onion mixture.

4 Place a large bowl over the top of the pan and turn the omelette out on to it, browned side up. Scrape off any bits adhering to the pan and heat 1 tablespoon olive oil in the pan. Then carefully slide the omelette back into the pan to brown the other side.

5 Slip the cooked omelette on to a heated serving plate, glaze with butter and garnish with sprigs of fresh watercress and quartered tomatoes. Serve immediately.

Cheese and Spring Onion Quiche

SERVES 6-8

225g/½ lb plain flour, sifted
1 tablespoon icing sugar
½ teaspoon salt
100g/1 ¼ lb cold butter
3 tablespoons freshly grated
  Parmesan cheese
2 tablespoons iced water
1 tablespoon lemon juice
1 egg yolk, beaten

Filling
4 egg yolks
300ml/½ pint single cream
150ml/¼ pint vegetable stock cube,
  crumbled
4 tablespoons white wine
4 tablespoons freshly grated Gruyère
Salt and freshly ground pepper
Freshly grated nutmeg
Cayenne pepper
6 tablespoons spring onion, finely sliced

To make pastry case:

1 Sift flour, icing sugar and salt into a large bowl. Cut cold butter into 5mm/¼inch squares and add to the bowl with freshly grated Parmesan cheese.

2 Using a pastry blender, or two knifes held scissor fashion one in each hand, cut diced butter and Parmesan cheese into flour mixture until it resembles coarse breadcrumbs.

4 Discard pastry blender or knifes. Scoop up some of the mixture in the palms of both hands and let it shower back lightly through your fingers, gently rubbing out the crumbs from between your fingertips. You should only need to do this six or seven times for the mixture to be reduced to fine breadcrumbs.

5 Sprinkle flour mixture with iced water and lemon juice and toss and mix pastry with a fork until about three quarters of the pastry is holding together. Then, use your hand, cupped, to press the pastry lightly into one piece.

6 Shape pastry into a round. Wrap in a sheet of greaseproof paper, followed by a dampened tea towel, and chill for at least 1 hour before using.

7 Roll out pastry and line a 23cm/ 9 inch pastry tin with removable bottom and bake blind in a preheated oven (400°F /200°C/ gas 6) for 10 minutes. Remove beans or rice, turn heat down to 350°F/180°C, gas 4 and return pastry case for just 5-8 minutes longer or until bottom crust is cooked.

To make filling:

1 Beat egg yolks in a bowl with single cream until well mixed. Add crumbled vegetable stock cube, dry white wine, freshly grated Gruyère and season with salt, ground pepper, freshly grated nutmeg and cayenne pepper, to taste. Stir in finely sliced spring onion.

2 Pour mixture into prepared pastry case and bake in a preheated 350°F/180°C/Gas 4 oven for 30-35 minutes. Serve immediately.

Quiche aux Fines Herbes

SERVES 6-8

1 25.5cm/10 inch pastry case, baked blind (see page 215)
4 eggs
1 egg white, beaten
150ml/½ pint double cream
150ml/½ pint milk
4 tablespoons freshly grated Parmesan
Salt
Freshly ground pepper
Crushed dried chillies

Freshly grated nutmeg
1 Spanish onion, finely chopped
2 tablespoons butter
1 'little gem' lettuce, cut into thin shreds
2 tablespoons each finely chopped chives, tarragon, parsley
½ teaspoon dried rosemary

Garnish:
Black olives
Sprigs of fresh herbs

To make quiche mixture:

1 In a medium sized bowl, beat eggs until light coloured. Fold in beaten egg white. Add double cream and milk and beat again.

2 Stir in freshly grated Parmesan cheese. Season with salt, freshly ground pepper and crushed dried chillies, to taste. Add a hint of freshly grated nutmeg.

3 In a medium-sized frying pan, sauté finely chopped onion in butter until transparent. Add shredded lettuce and heat through. Then add finely chopped herbs and dried rosemary. Remove from heat and stir in beaten egg and cream mixture.

When ready to bake quiche:

4 Fill pre-baked pastry case with quiche mixture and bake in a preheated oven (190°C/375°F/ Gas 5) for 40 minutes, or until quiche mixture is firm.

5 Garnish with black olives and sprigs of fresh herbs.

Cooking in Water

You can cook anything in water - from poached chicken to the *gigot à l'Irlandaise* of French classic cookery (a tender leg of mutton, boned and stuffed with herbs, then rolled in a suet pastry, wrapped carefully in a sheet of muslin and simmered gently in water until deliciously tender.).

Cooking in water does not, however, mean that you should not flavour it. Salt is, of course, used even when boiling a potato. But many cooks in France would never think of preparing their *bouillon* (the liquid in which everything is boiled) without adding a few peppercorns, a sprig of thyme or other herbs, a bay leaf, some onions, a little vinegar or equal quantities of wine and stock. I like to cook new potatoes, for instance, in a covered saucepan with just 1cm/½ inch water and 2-3 tablespoons butter or olive oil. Try this, too, with peas, spinach, carrots or sliced courgettes.

This addition of butter or oil makes all the difference, whether you are cooking a fish in a delicately prepared *court-bouillon* ; a fat, herb-stuffed chicken in rich stock spiked with dry white wine; or fresh egg noodles in a light white stock flavoured with a little olive oil and a touch of garlic.

Poaching

Other than when making tea or coffee, or cooking the occasional new potato, green vegetable or hard-boiled egg, I prefer to think of boiling in terms of poaching (a boiling that does not quite boil). 'Poaching' extends to all slow processes of cooking which involve the use of a liquid, no matter how small the quantity. Thus the term 'poach' applies equally to the cooking of a large fish (a turbot or salmon) in an aromatic *court-bouillon*, to fillets of sole simmered in a little fish *fumet*, or eggs or vegetables cooked in stock or water.

To poach fish

Whole fish or thick pieces of fish such as salmon, halibut, cod, ling, hake or turbot are best for poaching. Small fish or thin slices, steaks, or fillets to be cooked in liquid are better steamed, or 'poached' in the oven (see below).

Always put fish (except salt fish) into very hot water (not bubbling too hard), to which you have added 15g/½ oz salt and 1- 2 tablespoons vinegar or lemon juice per 2 litres/4 pints water.

A simple *court-bouillon* (quickly made stock) will lend extra savour if you add a bouquet garni (thyme, bay leaf and parsley), sliced carrots, onion and celery to the water, as well as salt and vinegar and lemon juice. For a more flavoursome court-bouillon, add ½ bottle inexpensive dry white wine, or half white wine and half water, instead of vinegar. If the fish tends to be dry, add 2 or more tablespoons olive oil.

A red *court-bouillon* can be made by substituting claret for the white wine to give the fish a bluish tinge.

A long, solid fish kettle with a drainer (to allow fish to be lifted out easily without breaking) is the best utensil for poaching fish. My kettle is 60cm/2 feet long, large enough to hold a young salmon or salmon trout comfortably. When poaching smaller fish or a centre cut of a larger fish I fasten the fish loosely to the drainer with a piece of string to prevent it floating around during cooking.

A large saucepan or flameproof casserole can be used for poaching fish. Place a plate on the bottom of the saucepan and on it put the fish, tied in a piece of muslin or cheesecloth, with the end of the cloth hanging over the sides of the pan so that the fish can be lifted out of the water easily without breaking.

Do not use too much liquid to cook the fish or the skin will probably break. Just enough liquid to cover the fish by 2.5-5cm/1-2 inches is a good rule. And if I use a proper fish poacher with a tight fitting lid, I use only enough *court-bouillon* to come halfway up the fish; the steam does the rest.

Allow the liquid to come to the boil again after the fish is put in; then reduce heat to a bare simmer and cook for the required time. If the fish is cooked too quickly, the outside will crack and break before the inside is ready. Remove all scum that rises; if allowed to remain it will spoil the appearance of the fish.

Test the fish by flaking it with a fork before it is lifted from the water. The flesh should have lost its clear appearance and be white and opaque. It should also come away from the bone easily; test by gently pushing in a wooden skewer. Do not overcook - overcooked fish is flavourless.

When the fish is ready, lift it out of the cooking liquid and drain well. If it needs to wait, keep warm on the drainer placed across the fish kettle and covered with a hot clean cloth. Garnish with fresh parsley and lemon wedges, and serve sauce separately. Boiled or steamed potatoes are usually served with boiled fish.

To pan-poach fish

One of the most delicate ways of cooking fish fillets and small fish steaks or cutlets is to pan-poach them in equal quantities of well-flavoured fish stock and dry white wine. Butter a shallow, heatproof gratin dish and place the fillets of fish in it. Season with salt, freshly ground pepper and a little lemon juice, and barely cover with fish stock and wine. Place a piece of well-buttered waxed paper over fish and cook in a hot oven (230°C/450°F/Gas 8) or on top of the stove until the fish is tender and opaque (about 8-12 minutes).

To oven-poach fish

The most effective method of poaching fish fillets isn't really poaching at all. It is oven-poaching, or poaching without liquid. Just place your fillets, or fish steaks, in a well-buttered, heatproof baking dish with a little finely chopped onion and mushroom, and salt and freshly ground pepper to taste. Cover the dish with buttered waxed paper or foil, and cook in the oven (190°C/375°F/Gas 5) until fish flakes with a fork. The fish may be served with or without sauce.

Aioli

SERVES 4-6

450g/1 lb salt codfish
6 white potatoes in their jackets
6 sweet potatoes in their jackets
6 courgettes
450g/1 lb small carrots
450g/1 lb French beans

6 hard-boiled eggs
6 ripe tomatoes
Lettuce
Fresh herbs (parsley, basil, chervil,
    chives etc), to decorate

1 Soak codfish overnight in cold water. Drain.

2 Put salt codfish in a saucepan, cover with cold water and bring to the boil; drain and return to the saucepan, cover with cold water and bring to the boil again. Turn off the heat and allow cod to steep in the hot water for 10 minutes. Remove cod from water and reserve.

3 Cook each vegetable separately, making sure they are tender but still quite firm and not over-cooked. Serve hot vegetables, hard-boiled eggs in their shells and raw tomatoes on large serving dishes decorated with lettuce and sprigs of fresh herbs. Place fish in centre. For best effect, group well-drained vegetables by colour. Serve with *aioli* sauce, from which this famous dish gets its name.

Aioli Sauce

4 fat cloves of garlic per person
Salt
1 egg yolk each for two persons

About 150ml/¼ pint olive oil for
    each yolk
Freshly ground pepper
Lemon juice

1 Crush the garlic to a smooth paste in a mortar with a little salt; blend in egg yolks until mixture is a smooth homogeneous mass. Now take the olive oil and proceed (drop by drop at first, a thin trickle later) to whisk the mixture as for a mayonnaise. The *aioli* will thicken gradually until it reaches the proper stiff, firm consistency. The exact quantity of olive oil is determined by the number of egg yolks used.

2 Season to taste with additional salt, a little freshly ground pepper and lemon juice. This sauce is served chilled in a bowl. Guests help themselves.

Poached Salmon in Court-Bouillon

SERVES 8-10

*1 whole salmon (about 1.8kg/4 lb),
    gutted and scaled*
Cucumber slices
Pimento strips
Aspic jelly

Garnish:
Boiled new potatoes
Sprigs of fresh mint

Court-Bouillon
2 litres/4 pints water
1 bottle dry white wine
1 fish stock cube
1 large Spanish onion, sliced
4 carrots, sliced
4 stalks celery, sliced
2 bay leaves
10 peppercorns
Salt
Bouquet garni

It is not that easy to poach a salmon really *well*. First of all, you need a fish poacher, with a removable rack, to allow you to lower the fish into the *court-bouillon* and, what's more important, to remove the fish without breaking it. And you need to measure your fish poacher, to be certain your salmon will fit into it.

1 Combine elements of *court-bouillon* in a fish poacher large enough to hold salmon. Bring to the boil, skim, lower heat and simmer for 20 minutes.

2 Let *court-bouillon* cool slightly. Place the cleaned salmon on the metal rack of the poacher, and lower the rack gently into *court-bouillon*. Return *court-bouillon* to the boil (about 3 minutes), then reduce heat to a simmer. Cover poacher and simmer salmon gently for 35-40 minutes, or until fish flakes easily with a fork.

3 Remove rack holding fish carefully from *court-bouillon*. Transfer the fish carefully to a board, using a large fish slice or spatula, and remove the skin with a sharp knife, leaving head and tail intact.

4 To serve cold: Arrange the salmon on a serving platter and garnish fish with overlapping 'scales' of paper-thin halved cucumber slices and 'fins' made of strips of cooked pimento. *Note*: I use tiny toothpicks to hold cucumber 'scales' to fish until aspic glaze holds them in place.

5 Brush fish with liquid aspic jelly. Allow jelly to set and then remove toothpicks. Serve with a well-flavoured mayonnaise.

Stuffed Fillets of Sole in Hollandaise Sauce

SERVES 4

2 sole, filleted
Softened butter
Salt and freshly ground pepper
4 tablespoons peeled prawns
2 shallots, finely chopped
Mushroom stalks and trimmings,
  chopped

¼ fish stock cube, crumbled
Fish bones and trimmings
4 baked pastry cases (see page 47)
1 recipe sauce Hollandaise
  (see page 33)

1 Lay fillets of sole out flat on a clean surface and brush with softened butter. Season with salt and freshly ground pepper. Place 1 level tablespoon prawns on each fillet and roll fillets up, starting from head. Fasten with toothpicks.

2 Place rolled fillets in a well-buttered *gratin* dish. Sprinkle with shallots, mushroom stalks and trimmings and crumbled fish stock cube, add salt and freshly ground pepper to taste, and cover with fish bones and trimmings. Cover with buttered paper and 'poach' in a preheated oven (230°C/450°F/Gas 8) for 10 minutes, or until fish flakes easily with a fork. Keep warm.

3 To serve fillets, place pastry cases on a baking tray and place 1 cooked fillet in each case. Spoon over sauce Hollandaise. Heat in a hot oven for a few minutes until the sauce bubbles.

Red Mullet with Fennel, Coriander & Basil 'Pistou'

SERVES 4

4 red mullet, scaled and cleaned

Court-bouillon
1 vegetable stock cube
2 small carrots, peeled and diced
8 green beans, diced
1 small white turnip, diced
1 potato, peeled and diced
1 red onion, peeled and diced
1 teaspoon fennel seeds
1 teaspoon coriander seeds
1 litre/2 pints water

Pistou Sauce
6-8 tablespoons olive oil
1-3 teaspoons balsamic vinegar
Crushed dried chillies
Sea salt
1-2 teaspoons fennel seeds
1-2 teaspoons chopped basil leaves

Garnish:
Sprigs of fresh basil

1 To prepare *court-bouillon*: Combine first 8 ingredients in a saucepan, add water and bring to the boil. Remove pan from heat until ready to cook.

2 Return pan to heat, add red mullets and bring to the boil. Cook for 1 minute and remove from the heat. Allow the fish to 'cook' in *bouillon* for 10 minutes (they will continue cooking in the heated water).

3 To prepare the *pistou* sauce to accompany red mullet: In a small bowl combine olive oil, balsamic vinegar, a pinch each of crushed dried chillies and sea salt. Add fennel seeds and chopped basil. Reserve.

4 Place the mullet on a serving dish, pour over the *pistou* sauce, garnish with basil and serve.

Sole in Creamy Saffron Sauce

SERVES 3-4

3-4 large fillets of sole

Court-bouillon
1 fish stock cube
600ml/1 pint water
Crushed dried chillies
Fennel seeds
Coriander seeds

Sauce
Crème fraîche
2 generous pinches of saffron

Garnish
Cooked sugar snap peas
Cooked broccoli florets
Cooked mangetout
Thinly sliced sun-dried tomatoes (in oil)

1 To prepare *court-bouillon*: In a shallow saucepan (large enough to contain sole fillets comfortably), combine fish stock cube and water. Add a pinch each of crushed, dried chillies, fennel and coriander seeds and bring to the boil.

2 Add the sole fillets, gently flattening each one with a wooden spoon or spatula as the fish cook in the *court-bouillon*. Bring gently to the boil over a medium heat, allow fish to cook for 1 minute more, then remove pan from the heat. The fish will gently cook in the hot *court-bouillon*.

3 To prepare the sauce: Transfer 150ml/¼ pint of the *court-bouillon* to a small saucepan. Cook over a high heat until it reduces to about 2 tablespoons. Add the *crème fraîche* to the pan with 2 generous pinches of saffron. Stir until the mixture is a creamy golden colour and coats the back of a spoon.

4 Return pan containing fish fillets to the heat. When hot, transfer fillets (using a fish slice) to a heated serving dish. Strain sauce over fish and garnish with cooked sugar snap peas, broccoli, mangetout and thinly sliced sun-dried tomatoes.

Chinese Steaming

Dim Sum – the traditional Chinese luncheon of little steamed delicacies in the individual bamboo streamer baskets in which they were cooked – is one of the most delightful ways of savouring Chinese cooking that I know.

Try steamed Shao Mai (tiny rounds of minced pork, water chestnuts and bean shoots folded in fragile won ton pastry leaves – see recipe below) or purchase a variety of Dim Sum at Chinese supermarkets and serve with a portion of rice noodles' Singapore (hair thin noodles sautéed with bits of roast pork, Chinese sausage, bean sprouts, shrimps, chilli and soy) or more simply steamed Chinese noodles (flavoured with a hint of sesame oil, lime juice and soy) for a meal to remember.

It is a fact that most Chinese home kitchens do not have or need an oven. Foods other than Dim Sum are often steamed in larger bamboo steaming baskets, now available in this country in Chinese supermarkets and some department stores. I have a selection of different sizes to steam thin strips of chicken, beef or pork flavoured with chopped ginger, garlic, spring onion and soy; and smaller ones to steam individual portions of scallops steamed in their shells with the above ingredients, plus mashed fermented black beans (see page 60). But I save my largest steamer for steaming red mullet, sea bass, or a medium-sized red snapper (see page 65) to create wonderfully healthy dishes with a unique flavour.

If you do not have a suitable bamboo steamer in your own kitchen and want to try your hand at Chinese steaming use a trivet or steamer tray inside your wok, or a shallow casserole with a lid, and pour in enough boiling water to come just below the rack on which the food stands. It is advisable to use plates that fit comfortably inside the steamer basket to hold the food to be steamed. Make sure that there is at least 1.75cm/2 inches free space between the plate and the edge of the steamer basket to allow the steam to circulate freely. This plate is necessary to catch the cooking juices.

When steaming a really large fish, I use my aluminium fish poacher, placing the perforated rack on three little heat-proof ramekins to keep it above the water in the poacher. In this case I make a base for my fish out of aluminium foil to catch the cooking juices. Quick steamed dishes can be made in a matter of minutes if you use fish, shellfish or tender strips of chicken, duck, pigeon, beef or pork.

Whole birds, or those cut into serving portions can be steamed in a tightly covered pan for longer cooking times. For these slow-cooked steamed dishes, the water used for steaming is often flavoured with spring onions, Chinese wine or soy to add savour to the steamed foods. Flavourful Chinese dipping sauces are usually served with this kind of dish; hot Chinese mustard, chilli sauce or soy to give a final fillip.

Note: For perfect steaming in the Chinese manner, make sure the plate is heated before the food is placed on it, and that the water is steaming before the plate is placed over that. This is very important because if the plate is not hot and the water is not steaming before the ingredient is placed in the steamer basket, the food will not really be steaming for the first few minutes of valuable cooking time, with a resulting loss of texture and flavour.

Chinese Steamed Scallops

SERVES 8 (or 4)

8 scallops, with half shells

For the sauce:
1 teaspoon cornflour dissolved in
  sake*
3 tablespoon sake* (or 1½ tbls each
  dry sherry and water)

2 tablespoons Chinese oyster sauce
2 tablespoons vegetable oil
2 tablespoons canned fermented
  black beans, drained
1.5 cm/½ inch fresh root ginger,
  peeled and very finely chopped
2 spring onions, finely chopped

1 Place the scallops, on their half shells, in a large bamboo steamer or in individual steamers; place steamer (or steamers) on a trivet in a wok (or in a large stockpot or fish poacher). Cover steamers and steam for 6-8 minutes. Remove steamer basket or baskets from heat. Reserve.

2 To make the sauce: in a small bowl mix together the cornflour (dissolved in sake or an equal quantity of dry sherry and water) with the oyster sauce to form a smooth paste. Reserve.

3 Heat the oil in a frying pan or wok, add the black beans and finely chopped ginger and spring onions and stir fry for 1 minute. Stir in the cornflour paste and cook for 1 minute more.

4 *To serve:* Pour a little of the sauce over each scallop in its half shell. Serve immediately.

* Available from some supermarkets and Chinese food stores

Steamed Dim Sum

Pork and Water Chestnut Shao Mai

(CHINESE DUMPLINGS WITH PORK AND WATER CHESTNUTS)

SERVES 2

6 frozen Shao Mai wrappers (won
ton skins)

Fillings:
225g/8 oz minced pork
1 teaspoon cornflour
4 water chestnuts*

1 canned bamboo shoot*
2 tablespoons chopped spring onion
½ teaspoon chopped fresh ginger
½ teaspoon salt
½ teaspoon sugar
crushed dried chillies

Defrost Shao Mai wrappers (won ton skins) and cover with a damp cloth. Let stand for 10 minutes.

To make the filling:
1 Place minced pork in a bowl; add cornflour and mix well.

2 Mince the water chestnuts and bamboo shoot separately.

To make Shao Mai dumplings:
1 Add the minced water chestnuts and bamboo shoot (step 2 above), chopped spring onion and chopped fresh ginger, salt and sugar. Add crushed dried chillies, to taste, and mix well.

2 Put a heaped teaspoon of the filling in the centre of each wrapper (or skin) and pinch lightly together, leaving a small opening at the top of each wrapper (or skin) to show filling.

3 Place the Shao Mai dumplings on a heated plate over rack in steamer and steam for 30 minutes. Serve hot with side dishes of soy sauce and Chinese mustard.

* Available from some supermarkets and Chinese food stores

Chinese Steamed Vegetables

SERVES 2-4

100g/4 oz mange tout
(or sugar snap peas)
100g/4 oz baby corn
60g/2 oz shitake mushrooms
2 small courgettes, cut into strips
the same size as the corn and
green beans
½ red pepper, cored, seeded and
sliced

½ yellow (or orange) pepper, cored, seeded
and sliced
4 spring onions, cut into 50mm/3 inch
segments
4 tablespoons vegetable oil
Crushed dried chillies
2-4 teaspoons soy sauce
Lime juice, sake* or mirin*

1 On a shallow plate in a bamboo steamer, combine all the vegetables and steam for five minutes, or until tender.

2 Just before serving, season with a sauce made of vegetable oil seasoned with crushed dried chillies, soy sauce and lime juice, or sake, or mirin, to taste.

Chinese Steamed Noodles

SERVES 2

100g/4 oz Chinese noodles
Boiling water
2-4 teaspoons sake* (or equal quantity of dry sherry and water)
2-4 teaspoons soy sauce

1 Put the noodles in a bowl, and pour over boiling water, to cover. Allow noodles to soak for 3 to 4 minutes.

2 Place noodles in the bamboo steamer and steam for 5 minutes, or until tender. Season with sake (or equal quantity of dry sherry mixed with water) and soy sauce.

* Available from some supermarkets and Chinese food stores

Steamed Red Snapper with Garlic, Ginger and Spring Onions

SERVES 2

1 medium sized red snapper (choose fish to fit comfortably in your steamer) or 2 fat steaks of red snapper
Salt
Lemon juice
3 cloves garlic, finely sliced
2 spring onions, finely sliced
2.5cm/ 1inch fresh ginger, peeled and finely sliced
2 tablespoons light soy sauce

2 tablespoons mirin* (Japanese rice wine) or 1 tablespoon each of dry sherry and water
1 teaspoon sesame oil
6 tablespoons peanut or vegetable oil
2 tablespoons chopped fresh coriander

Garnish:
Spring onion 'tassles'
Thin rings of red and yellow pepper

1 To prepare the fish (whole snapper or snapper steaks): if using a whole snapper make 3 incisions along each side. Rub the fish (or fish steaks) with salt and lemon juice on both sides

2 Place a shallow dish in the bamboo steamer, leaving enough space on all sides to allow steam to circulate.

3 Place fish on plate in steamer. Sprinkle with finely sliced garlic, spring onions and ginger. Pour over soy sauce, mirin and sesame oil. Cover steamer and place over rapidly boiling water for 15 minutes.

4 Transfer the fish to a heated serving plate. Heat the peanut or vegetable oil to boiling in a small saucepan and pour over the fish. Then sprinkle with the finely chopped coriander.

5 Garnish with spring onion 'tassles' and pepper rings. Serve immediately.

* Available from some supermarkets and Chinese food stores

Chinese Steamed Chicken

SERVES 4

1 roasting chicken (1.6 kg/3½ lb)
½ lemon
Salt and freshly ground pepper
2 tablespoons vegetable oil
2 tablepoons sake* or mirin*
2 tablespoons soy sauce

4 tablespoons chicken stock
2 tablespoons finely chopped onion
2 tablespoons finely chopped coriander
2 tablespoons finely sliced spring onions
Crushed dried chillies

1 Rub cleaned and trussed chicken with cut side of ½ lemon. Sprinkle with salt and freshly ground pepper to taste. Place in a *gratin* dish just large enough to hold it.

2 Add vegetable oil, sake or mirin, soy sauce, chicken stock and finely chopped onion to *gratin* dish. Place dish in a large double steamer over 7cm/3 inches rapidly boiling water. Cover steamer and steam for 1-1¼ hours or until chicken is cooked through.

3 Serve chicken with pan juices to which you have added finely chopped coriander leaves, thinly sliced spring onion and crushed dried chillies, to taste.

* Available from some supermarkets and Chinese food stores

Chinese Steamed Prawns

SERVES 4

700g/1½ lb frozen prawns
Cornflour
4 shallots, finely chopped
100g/4oz mushrooms, finely sliced
50g/2 oz cucumber, finely sliced

4 tablespoons soy sauce
4 tablespoons dry white wine
Freshly ground pepper
Rice
Tomatoes

1 Defrost prawns. Roll in cornflour and place on a platter in steamer* with finely chopped shallots, finely sliced mushrooms and cucumber, soy sauce and white wine. Season with freshly ground pepper, and cook over 5cm/2 inches fast-boiling water, covered (so platter is entirely confined in steam), until tender.

* If you do not have a steamer, place a trivet in the bottom of a casserole large enough to contain platter and cook, covered, over fast-boiling water.

2 Serve hot from the steamer on a bed of rice, garnished with fresh tomatoes.

Cooking With Wine

Cooking with wine is as easy as opening a bottle and taking a sip. If, like some of my friends, you are a little inhibited in your use of this magic cook's aid, think of it as just another ingredient like butter, olive oil, fresh herbs or cream.

'Take 900g-1.4kg/ 2-3 lb of an inexpensive cut of meat. Cut into 3.5-4cm/1½-1¾ inch slices; dust the pieces generously with flour, salt and freshly ground pepper and sauté in equal quantities of olive oil and butter in a large, heatproof casserole until the meat is browned on all sides. Remove meat from the casserole and reserve. Simmer some coarsely chopped onion and garlic in the same combination of fats; return meat to the casserole and combine with the vegetables; add strips of orange peel which you have dried in the oven, 2 cloves, 2 bay leaves and a reduction of red wine. Cover the casserole and simmer gently over the lowest of heats, until the meat is meltingly tender and the vegetables and wine dissolve into a smooth, richly flavoured sauce.'

This easy casserole recipe probably originated centuries ago on the sun-washed hillsides of southern France, when the natives of the region were learning how to cultivate the local grapes to make wine. The casserole was undoubtedly cooked in the ashes. Today the task is easier, but all the magic 'constants' remain.

Slow, even cooking

All casseroles - meats, poultry, fish, game and vegetables – respond wonderfully well to 'low heat' cookery. Over the many years I have been experimenting with heat I have gradually lowered the temperature at which I like to cook stews, daubes, ragoûts and casseroles to 110°C/225°F/Gas ¼ or 140°C/275°F/Gas 1. When cooking this type of dish on top of the stove I always use an asbestos or wire mat to help keep the cooking down to a very faint, barely perceptible simmer. The first few times you follow this method of cooking, check on your casserole frequently – thermostats vary, and you may find you have to adjust the setting slightly to keep the casserole at a low 'barely simmering' point. Always bring the ingredients up to a bubble on top of the stove before you put the casserole in the oven.

Reduction

Wine 'reduced' to a quarter of the original quantity by a fast boil over a high heat is one of the best ways of adding savour to a casserole. Professional cooks use this method of seasoning to intensify the depth of flavour of their wine simmered dishes.

I like to reduce stock in the same manner, adding a combination of two separate reductions to the dish at the last minute – (1) a reduction of stock and (2) a reduction of wine – to give hidden depth and interest to a ragoût of meat, poultry or game. Try combining separate reductions of fish stock and dry white wine to add excitement to a fish soup, casserole or fish-based cream or velouté sauce.

Small quantities of wine can make a great difference to your cooking.

Red wine marinade

Ingredients for Boeuf Bourguignon

White Wine Fish Stock (Fumet de Poisson)

900g/2lb fish heads and bones
1 Spanish onion, sliced
4 carrots, sliced
2 stalks celery, sliced
4 tablespoons olive oil

900ml/1½ pints dry white wine
Dash of dried fennel
4 parsley sprigs
2 bay leaves
Salt and freshly ground pepper

1 Chop fish heads and bones into pieces about 7cm/3 inches long. Combine chopped bones and sliced vegetables in a large heatproof casserole and sauté in olive oil, stirring constantly, until vegetables begin to colour. Add dry white wine and 900ml/1½ pints water and bring to the boil.

2 Skim surface of stock. Add fennel, parsley and bay leaves. Simmer for 2 hours.

3 Strain stock through a fine sieve lined with muslin. Season with salt and freshly ground black pepper, to taste.

Red or White Wine Marinade (For fish, chicken or meat)

1 bottle full-bodied red or white
  wine
2 Spanish onions, thinly sliced
2 large carrots, thinly sliced
2 stalks celery, thinly sliced
1 clove garlic, peeled

2 sprigs parsley
1 sprig thyme
1 bay leaf
2-4 tablespoons olive oil
8-10 black peppercorns

Combine marinade ingredients in a large bowl and mix well. Cover bowl tightly with foil and leave overnight in a cool place before using to marinate meats, fish, poultry or game. You will find that leaving the marinade ingredients overnight will add immeasurably to the ultimate flavour of the dish.

Halibut in Champagne

SERVES 4

4 turbot fillets, boned and skinned
¼ fish stock cube
100g/4oz butter
2 tablespoons olive oil
2 shallots, finely chopped
100g/4oz button mushrooms, sliced

6 tablespoons reduced* fish stock made
  from fish trimmings
½ quarter bottle of champagne
Salt and white pepper
150ml/¼ pint double cream
1 tablespoon cornflour

1 Melt half the butter in a large shallow saucepan with olive oil. Add ¼ crumbled fish stock cube and sauté finely chopped shallots until transparent,then add sliced mushrooms and continue cooking until tender. Remove.

2 Add remaining butter to pan and sauté turbot fillets until lightly coloured. Add sautéed mushrooms and onions, fish stock and half the champagne, adding more if necessary barely to cover the turbot fillets. Season to taste with salt and white pepper and simmer very slowly for a few minutes until tender. Remove fish to a serving dish and keep warm.

3 Add cream to the liquid in the pan and simmer without boiling until cream is warm. Mix cornflour with a small amount of water, add to sauce and cook, stirring constantly, over a very low heat, until sauce is smooth and rich.

4 When ready to serve, pour in remaining champagne, stir and mix with the sauce until warm. If you prefer a thicker sauce, use less champagne. Pour over turbot fillets and serve immediately.

* To reduce fish stock: in a small saucepan, combine fish bones and trimmings with 1 slice onion and 1 bay leaf and 200ml/8fl oz water and cook over a high heat until reduced to about one-third of the original quantity. Strain and use as above.

Halibut in Champagne

Classic Coq au Vin

Classic Coq Au Vin

SERVES 4-6

For the marinade:
½ bottle good red wine
2 carrots, sliced
1 Spanish onion, sliced
2 bay leaves
2 cloves garlic
2 stalks celery, sliced

For the chicken:
1 roasting chicken
 (about ½kg/3½lbs) cut into
 6 or 8 serving pieces
2 tablespoons butter
2 tablespoons lard

2 tablespoons olive oil
100g/½ lb salt pork, in
 1 piece
12 button onions
12 button mushrooms
Flour
Salt and freshly ground
 pepper
Crushed dried chillies
2 cloves garlic, finely chopped
1 sprig thyme
2 bay leaves
2 sprigs parsley

To finish the casserole:
4 tablespoons cognac
1 sugar lump
1 tablespoon flour
1 tablespoon butter
2 tablespoons finely
 chopped parsley

Garnish:
Snippets of fried bread
Finely chopped parsley

1 To marinate chicken pieces: place chicken pieces in a large, shallow bowl: pour over red wine and add aromatics of the marinade. For the utmost flavour, leave the chicken to marinate in the wine and aromatics overnight.

2 When ready to cook, heat 2 tablespoons each butter, lard and olive oil in a large heat proof casserole with the salt pork (cut into 'finger' lengths).

3 When the pork begins to turn golden, add the button onions and cook for a few minutes, or until the onions begin to turn transparent. Then add the button mushrooms and continue cooking, stirring until the mushrooms begin to change colour. Remove salt pork 'fingers', button onions and mushrooms from pan and reserve.

4 To cook the chicken: Preheat the oven to 140°C/275°F/Gas 1. Remove the chicken pieces from the marinade with a slotted spoon (reserving marinade for later use). Pat the chicken pieces dry with a paper towel, then roll them in flour and sauté them in the fats left in the pan for about 5 minutes, or until they turn golden brown on one side. Then, without piercing them, turn the chicken pieces to brown on the other side. As each piece begins to 'stiffen' remove it and put it in a shallow bowl in the preheated oven. When all the chicken pieces have been browned, return the onions, salt pork, mushrooms, chicken pieces and their juices to the casserole. Add salt, freshly ground pepper, crushed dried chillies, finely chopped garlic, thyme, bay leaves and parsley. Strain the marinade juices over the contents of the casserole; cover and cook in the preheated oven for 45 minutes, or until chicken is tender.

5 Remove chicken pieces, salt pork and vegetables from the casserole and keep warm. Skim off excess fat from the juices in the casserole. Set casserole on a high heat, pour in cognac (warmed in a soup ladle over direct heat) and ignite, standing well back from the burning alcohol. Allow to burn for a minute or two and then add a lump of sugar; bring to the boil and reduce the sauce over a high heat to half the original quantity.

6 Thicken the sauce with a *beurre manie* made of the remaining 1 tablespoon butter and tablespoon flour. Strain sauce into a clean casserole; return chicken pieces, salt pork and vegetables to the casserole; cover and let simmer in the lowest of ovens until it is time to serve. Garnish with snippets of fried bread and chopped parsley.

Boeuf Bourguignon

SERVES 4

900g/2 lb beef
½ bottle red wine
225g/8oz carrots, sliced
25g/1 oz shallots, finely chopped
50g/2 oz onions, finely chopped
2-4 cloves garlic
1-2 sprigs thyme
1-2 bay leaves
6 peppercorns
Olive oil
Butter

Flour
1 glass water
Bouquet garni
225g/8 oz bacon, diced

Garnish
12 baby carrots, blanched
12 button onions, blanched
12 button mushrooms
Salt and freshly ground pepper
Butter

1 Cut beef into bite-sized pieces and marinate overnight in red wine with carrots, shallots, onion, garlic, thyme, bay leaves and peppercorns. Drain well.

2 Preheat the oven to 140°C/275°F/Gas 1. Sauté drained beef in 1 tablespoon each olive oil and butter until lightly browned.

3 Sprinkle with 1-2 tablespoons flour; add the red wine marinade, the water and the bouquet garni.

4 Cover casserole and cook beef in the preheated oven for 2¾-3 hours or until the sauce is reduced by half and the meat is tender.

5 In a large, thick-bottomed frying pan or shallow heatproof casserole, sauté the diced bacon and garlic in 2 tablespoons butter.

6 Add the blanched carrots, button onions and 4 tablespoons water to the frying pan and cook over a moderate heat until tender.

7 Add the mushrooms and continue to cook, stirring from time to time, until mushrooms are cooked.

8 Serve the Bourguignon garnished with the glazed bacon and vegetables.

Sole with Vermouth

SERVES 4

8 fillets of sole, skinned
Softened butter
Salt and freshly ground pepper
8 tablespoons dry vermouth

4 tablespoons melted butter
1-2 teaspoons tomato puree
6-8 tablespoons creme fraiche
1 bunch of watercress to garnish

1 Butter a shallow, heatproof frying pan or gratin dish. Season the sole fillets with salt and freshly ground pepper and arrange them in the buttered pan.

2 In a bowl, blend together the vermouth, melted butter and tomato purée and pour the mixture over the sole.

3 Place the pan over a medium heat and bring to the boil, then reduce the heat, and poach the fish very gently for 4-5 minutes, until the fish is cooked.

4 With a fish slice, remove the cooked sole from the dish and arrange on a heated serving dish. Keep warm.

5 Add the crème fraîche to the sauce in the pan and heat through, stirring, until the sauce has thickened. Strain the sauce over the fish. Garnish with 'bouquets' of watercress and serve immediately.

Grilling

To grill food is to cook it quickly by direct heat over charcoal or under gas or electricity. Because of its speed, grilling can go horribly wrong: A minute too long and the end result is ruined. Thick cuts of meat or fish should be cooked at a greater distance from the heat, thinner cuts, closer to the heat. Always ensure that the metal grid of the grill is hot before you start grilling.

Open-fire grilling

One of the hazards of open-fire grilling is that fat dripping from the meat causes the fire to flare up and smoke. So keep coals under the meat for a short time until the meat browns, then spread them in a circle with none directly under the meat. If flames still flare up, put a dripping pan under the meat.

If you want a fire that sears quickly (perfect for grilling small fish, minute steaks or skewered meats) the charcoal should be piled about two or three inches high. If you need a lazy, more controlled heat for a whole leg of lamb or a large duck, the charcoal should be spread out in a single layer, with the coals separated a little from each other.

Keep a circle of fresh charcoal at the outer edge of your fire and push it into the centre as needed. A bulb syringe filled with water should be kept handy to tame flames when necessary.

It is important not to start cooking too soon. For perfect grilling, charcoal should look ash-grey by day and have a warm, red glow after dark. If your charcoal is still flaming, it is too early to start cooking.

Grilling meat over an open fire

Always give meat on the spit or grill a chance to warm up and relax over the coals before you start basting. The meat will absorb the flavours of your basting sauce better this way. A word to the wise: if your sauce has a tomato base, do not use it until the last 15 minutes of cooking time. This gives a rosy brown glaze to barbecued meats and avoids unnecessary scorching.

Grilling under gas or electricity

Practice will teach you how to deal most successfully with your own grill. One easy rule to remember: thick cuts of meat and fish should be cooked at a greater distance from the heat, thinner cuts, near the heat.

To grill steaks or chops successfully: season meat with freshly ground pepper and place on preheated grid. The thicker cuts of meat should be 'seized' on both sides with a very high heat to preserve their juices, before cooking at a more moderate heat to allow its gradual penetration into the juicy centre of the meat. The smaller cuts (tournedos, chops, cutlets) can be cooked without lowering the heat once the juices have been sealed in. For best results, season meats with salt after cooking.

Brochettes of Halibut or Turbot

SERVES 6

700g/1 ½ lb halibut or turbot (thick end of fillet)
4 firm medium-sized tomatoes, sliced
3 small onions, sliced
Rice or shredded lettuce

Basting Sauce
8 tablespoons olive oil
4 tablespoons dry white wine
½ Spanish onion, finely chopped
2 bay leaves, crumbled
Salt and freshly ground pepper

1 To make basting sauce: Combine olive oil, dry white wine, finely chopped onion, crumbled bay leaves and salt and freshly ground pepper, to taste, in a large shallow bowl.

2 Cut halibut or turbot into chunks (2-3 cm/ ¾-1¼ inches square). You should have about 30 in all - any thin pieces should be rolled up into pieces the same size as chunks.

3 Slice tomatoes and onions ½ cm/¼ inch thick.

4 Place fish pieces in bowl with basting sauce. Toss fish carefully in sauce; cover half the bowl with slices of tomato and the other half with slices of onion. Place bowl in the refrigerator for at least 2 hours.

5 When ready to cook, thread six 20 or 22½ cm/8 or 9 inch metal skewers with alternate pieces of fish and tomato and onion slices, starting and ending with a chunk of fish, and dividing the ingredients equally between skewers.

6 Line rack of grill pan with foil. Arrange skewers on it; brush with half the basting sauce and place under a preheated hot grill. Reduce heat to moderate and grill for 4-5 minutes.

7 Turn skewers; baste with remaining sauce and continue to grill for 4-5 minutes longer, or until fish flakes easily with a fork. Serve immediately on a bed of rice or shredded lettuce, spooning some of the cooking juices over skewers.

Charcoal-grilled Chuletas

SERVES 4-6

4-6 sirloin steaks, 2.5cm/1 inch
  thick
8 tablespoons olive oil
4 tablespoons dry white wine
1 tablespoon lemon juice
2 tablespoons coarsely chopped
  onion

2 cloves garlic, chopped
¼ teaspoon rubbed oregano
¼ teaspoon crumbled bay leaves
1 tablespoon chopped parsley
1 piece of fresh beef suet
Salt and freshly ground pepper

1 Remove meat from the refrigerator at least 30 minutes before cooking. Pierce holes all over the surface of the steaks with a thick barbecue skewer.

2 Combine remaining 10 ingredients and brush steaks with this mixture, forcing it well down into holes in meat. Allow meat to marinate for at least 2 hours before cooking.

3 To grill: Rub hot grid with a piece of suet, place steaks on grid and brush with marinade. Grill over charcoal for 5 minutes on each side for a rare steak, a few minutes longer if you prefer your steak medium rare. Season generously with salt and freshly ground pepper.

These may be spread on hot steak before serving.

Devil Spread

Cream 1 tablespoon Worcestershire sauce and 4 drops Tabasco with 100g/4oz butter.

Roquefort Spread

Cream 50g/2oz Roquefort cheese with a 100g/4oz butter.

Mustard Spread

Cream 4 tablespoons Dijon mustard with 100g/4oz butter.

Grilled Rump or Sirloin

SERVES 4

*1 large rump steak (about
3 cm/1 ½ inches thick) or 4 small
sirloin steaks (225g/8oz each)
Freshly ground pepper*

*4 tablepoons butter
Olive oil (optional)
Cracked peppercorns (optional)
Salt*

1 Remove meat from refrigerator at least 30 minutes before cooking. Trim off excess fat and score remaining fat in several places around side to prevent meat from curling up during cooking.

2 Preheat grill for 15-20 minutes.

3 Either sprinkle both sides of steak (or steaks), with freshly ground pepper and spread with 4 tablespoons softened butter; or brush steak (or steaks) on both sides with olive oil seasoned with cracked peppercorns.

4 Rub hot grill with a piece of excess fat. Place steak (or steaks) on grid, and grill for 6-8 minutes on each side for a rare steak, brushing with melted butter or olive oil from time to time. Grill a few minutes longer if you prefer steak to be medium rare. Sprinkle with salt to taste.

Grilled Lamb with Oriental Spices

SERVES 6

1.25kg/2½ lb lamb, cut from leg
Salt and freshly ground pepper
2 teaspoons coriander
2 teaspoons cumin seed
1 Spanish onion, finely chopped

2 teaspoons brown sugar
4 tablespoons soy sauce
4 tablespoons lemon juice
¼ teaspoon powdered ginger

1 Cut lamb into 2.5cm/1 inch cubes and combine in a porcelain bowl with remaining ingredients. Mix well and marinate lamb cubes in this mixture for at least 4 hours, turning lamb from time to time so that it absorbs all the flavours.

2 When ready to grill, drain and reserve marinade and thread meat on to skewers, 4-6 cubes on each. Brush with marinade and grill for 5 minutes about 7cm/3 inches from the coals. Turn lamb and baste with marinade every 5 minutes until done, around 20-25 minutes in all.

Spatch-Cocked Chicken

SERVES 4

2 tender young chickens
(1kg/2-2½lb each)
Salt, freshly ground pepper and
paprika
Lemon juice
Melted butter
6 tablespoons breadcrumbs,
browned in 2 tablespoons butter, or
4 tablespoons finely chopped thyme,
tarragon and parsley
Sprigs of watercress and lemon wedges

To garnish:
Grilled half tomatoes
Pepper rings

1 Split cleaned chickens open through the back, flatten out and trim birds, cutting off feet and wing tips. Wipe with a damp cloth, and season generously with salt, freshly ground pepper, paprika and a little lemon juice.

2 Skewer birds open and brush both sides with melted butter. Sprinkle with fine brown breadcrumbs, or chopped herbs.

3 Place the birds, (bone sides down) on grill pan, over charcoal (or bone sides up under grill) and cook for 10 minutes. Then turn them over and continue to cook for 15-20 minutes more, turning the birds occasionally and basting frequently with melted butter. Serve very hot, garnished with watercress, lemon wedges, grilled half tomatoes and pepper rings.

Grilled Chicken with Lemon and Garlic

SERVES 4-6

1 roasting chicken
100g/4oz butter
Grated rind and juice of 1 lemon
2 cloves garlic, finely chopped
½ level teaspoon dried oregano

2 tablespoons olive oil
Salt and freshly ground pepper
2 tablespoons finely chopped
  parsley

1 Cut chicken into serving pieces. Place chicken pieces in a generously buttered, shallow heatproof baking dish. Sprinkle with grated lemon rind, finely chopped garlic and dried oregano and pour over strained lemon juice and olive oil. Flavour to taste with salt and freshly ground pepper. Dot with remaining butter and refrigerate for at least 2 hours.

2 Preheat grill and cook chicken under it for about 15 minutes, basting frequently with marinade juices, until chicken pieces are brown on one side. Turn pieces over and grill on other side until well browned.

3 Remove baking dish from under the grill and baste chicken pieces with pan juices. Cover the baking dish (or cover chicken pieces with aluminium foil) and continue to cook in a preheated oven (170°C/325°F/Gas 3) for 30–40 minutes, or until chicken is tender, basting from time to time. Sprinkle with finely chopped parsley and serve immediately.

Magret de Canard au Poivre Vert

SERVES 4

4 breasts of duck
Butter
Salt and freshly ground pepper
2 tart eating apples, thinly sliced
Green peppercorns
Sprigs of watercress

Glace de Canard
Carcass and trimmings of duck
¼ chicken stock cube
1 tablespoon tomato purée
1 carrot, finely chopped
½ Spanish onion, finely chopped
6 tablespoons butter
150ml/¼ pint dry white wine
Freshly ground pepper

1 To prepare *glace de canard*: Chop duck carcass and trimmings coarsely. Combine ¼ chicken stock cube and tomato purée with carrot and onion and sauté in butter until ingredients are well browned. Add 600ml/1 pint water and wine and cook, skimming from time to time, until sauce is reduced to half its original quantity. Strain sauce into a small saucepan, pressing vegetables and bones to extract all juice. Continue to cook sauce over a low heat until it is reduced to about 150ml/¼ pint. Season with freshly ground pepper, to taste. Reserve.

2 Brush duck breasts with melted butter and season generously with salt and freshly ground pepper, to taste. Grill for 10 minutes on each side.

3 Remove skin from duck breasts(using a kitchen towel to protect your hands). Keep duck breast warm.

4 Place duck breasts on a heatproof serving dish or shallow casserole (an oval enamelled iron *gratin* dish is good as it can go directly on to the heat). Keep warm in oven. In the meantime, sauté apple slices in butter until golden brown. Make a new 'skin' for each breast of duck by covering with overlapping apple slices.

5 Place gratin dish on a medium heat and heat duckling. Brush apple slices with a little *glace de canard*; add 1-2 tablespoons green peppercorns to remainder and pour around duck breasts in pan. Garnish with watercress and serve at once.

Pan Grilled Red Mullet in Vine Leaves

Pan Grilling

An excellent method of grilling steaks at home is to grill them in an iron frying pan brushed with a little fat or in one of the special grill pans made for this purpose. Season meat to taste with freshly ground pepper, sear quickly on one side, reduce the heat and cook for a minute or two longer. Turn the meat, sear on the other side and continue cooking and turning until it is done to your taste.

Beef

Beef is the most popular meat for grilling. The best cuts to use for grilling are the fillet, rump and the upper cut of sirloin. I like a good thick rib steak, cut from the sirloin, complete with bone. The most expensive cuts of beef for grilling are those cut from the fillet, usually named according to their thickness: a tournedos is a small piece of fillet about 3.5cm/ 1¾ inches thick; the famous *filet mignon* is a piece 4.5 cm/1½-2 inches thick; while a piece 5-7.5 cm/ 2-3 inches thick is known as a *Châteaubriant* .

White meats

When grilling white meats (veal, lamb or chicken) a moderate heat will ensure that you cook and colour the meat simultaneously. Baste white-meat grills fairly often with butter, or butter and olive oil. They are done when the juices run clear and colourless.

To grill fish

Wash and clean fish. Dry lightly and score the skin across diagonally on both sides to prevent it cracking during cooking. Season with salt and freshly ground pepper, and brush with olive oil or melted butter. Or marinate fish for 2 hours before cooking in equal quantities of olive oil and dry white wine with a little finely chopped garlic and a crumbled bay leaf or two. Or split open the fish, remove the bones, then lightly coat the fish with flour, egg and breadcrumbs, or fine oatmeal.

   For best results, heat the pan thoroughly and grease it well before you place the fish on it. Cook fish for 8-12 minutes according to thickness, and turn at least once during the cooking time. I serve grilled fish with lemon quarters and *fines herbes* butter (beaten with finely chopped parsley, chives, tarragon and a hint of marjoram and lemon juice).

Pan-grilled Red Mullet in Vine Leaves

SERVES 4

4 small red mullet, or sole
Salt and Lemon juice
Juice of ½ orange
1 teaspoon crushed coriander seeds
Freshly ground pepper

Crushed dried chillies
8 fresh vine leaves or banana leaves
Olive oil
Lemon slices
Sprigs of fresh watercress

1 Thoroughly clean the fish, removing fins, scales and insides, but leaving the heads and tails intact. Rub the insides of fish with salt and lemon juice; leave for 30 seconds, then wash well and pat dry.

2 Mix the orange juice with 2 tablespoons olive oil, crushed coriander seeds, salt, freshly ground pepper and crushed dried chillies, to taste.

3 Make a few slashes across the fish on both sides with a sharp knife; rub the orange marinade juices into the fish. Wrap each fish in 2 vine leaves (or squares of banana leaves) and fix with 4 cocktail sticks. Reserve

4 Heat the grill pan until a drop of oil or water sizzles on contact with the hot pan. Pan grill the fish for 10-12 minutes, turning once. Serve immediately, garnished with lemon slices and slices of fresh watercress.

Pan-grilled Hamburgers with Sauce Bordelaise

SERVES 4

*1kg/ 2lb minced rump or
  sirloin steak
4 tablespoons very finely chopped
  beef marrow, or beef fat
1 small onion, finely chopped*

*4 tablespoons finely chopped chives
Salt and freshly ground pepper
Olive oil
2 tablespoons finely chopped parsley
Sauce Bordelaise (prepared in advance)*

1 In a medium sized mixing bowl, combine the minced beef steak with the very finely chopped beef marrow (or beef fat) and the finely chopped onion and chives. Season with salt and freshly ground pepper to taste and mix ingredients as lightly as possible. The secret of a tender, moist hamburger is to touch the minced meat as little as possible when mixing it.

2 When ready to cook, lightly form the mixture into 4 patties about 10cm/4 inches in diameter. Brush the grill pan with olive oil and heat the pan over a high heat until the oil sizzles. Place the patties in the pan and cook for 2½ minutes on each side over a high heat. This gives the patties a crisp finish, while the interior stays meltingly rare and moist. If you prefer the hamburgers a little more cooked, lower heat and cook for 1-2 minutes longer.

3 When ready to serve, transfer hamburgers to a heated serving dish and keep warm. Bring sauce Bordelaise to the boil and spoon a little over each hamburger. Sprinkle with finely chopped parsley and serve remaining sauce separately.

To make the sauce Bordelaise:
In a small saucepan, sauté 2 finely chopped shallots in 2 tablespoons butter with ½ chicken stock cube until shallots are transparent. Add 170ml/6fl oz red wine and cook until liquid is reduced to ¼ of its original quantity. Add ½ pint well-flavoured brown sauce and simmer gently for 10 minutes. Remove the marrow from a 5cm/2 inch split beef bone; cut it into small dice and poach diced marrow in boiling salted water for 1-2 minutes. Drain and, just before serving, add the diced beef marrow and a little finely chopped parsley to the sauce.

Pan Grilled Hamburger with Sauce Bordelaise

Pan Grilled Strip Sirloin with Tapenade

Pan-grilled Strip Sirloin Steaks with Tapenade

SERVES 4

4 tender sirloin strip steaks
Olive oil
Freshly ground pepper
Softened butter
Salt
Crushed dried chillies

Tapenade (black olive sauce,
*   available in supermarkets)*

Garnish:
Grilled half tomatoes
Lemon slices

1 Remove steaks from the refrigerator at least 30 minutes before grilling and slit fat in several places around sides of steaks to prevent meat from curling up during cooking.

2 Brush grill pan with olive oil and heat pan over a high heat until oil sizzles.

3 When ready to cook steaks: sprinkle steaks on both sides with freshly ground pepper and spread with a little softened butter.

4 Place steaks on a hot grill pan and grill for 3 minutes on each side for rare; cook a few minutes more if you prefer steaks to be medium rare.

5 Sprinkle steaks with a pinch each of salt and crushed dried chillies, to taste and serve immediately accompanied by tapenade.

Pan-grilled Marinated Lamb Steaks

SERVES 2

2 lamb steaks, cut from leg of lamb
4 tablespoons olive oil
4 tablespoons lemon juice
2 teaspoons ground cumin

1 teaspoon ground coriander
Freshly ground pepper
Coarse salt

1 Place lamb steaks in a shallow *gratin* dish or baking pan.

2 Mix olive oil and lemon juice and pour over steaks. Sprinkle both sides of steaks with ground cumin, coriander and freshly ground pepper to taste. Rub spices in well. Cover dish with aluminium foil and refrigerate for 12-24 hours, turning steaks once or twice during this time so that they absorb all the flavours.

3 When ready to cook, heat iron grill pan over medium heat until it is very hot. Place steaks on grill pan and grill for 3-5 minutes on one side. Season with coarse salt to taste. Turn steaks, brush with marinade and grill on other side for 3-5 minutes. Test meat for 'doneness' by cutting into edge of steak to check colour. Serve immediately.

Pan-grilled Lamb's Kidneys en Brochette

SERVES 4

8-12 lamb's kidneys
4-6 tablespoons melted butter
Salt and freshly ground pepper
Fresh breadcrumbs
Olive oil

Garlic butter
4 slices grilled bacon
Sprigs of watercress

1 Split kidneys in half from rounded edge and remove thin outer skin. Open and run skewer through them to keep them open. Brush kidneys with melted butter, season with salt and freshly ground pepper, and sprinkle generously with breadcrumbs.

2 Heat a large, heavy-bottomed grill pan over a moderately high heat until drops of water shaken on to the surface bounce and sizzle on contact. Brush ridges of grill pan with olive oil and grill kidneys until cooked through. Do not overcook or kidneys will be tough.

3 Just before serving, place a row of garlic butter on each kidney half. Garnish with grilled bacon and sprigs of watercress. Serve with boiled new potatoes.

Garlic Butter

¼ b butter, slightly softened
1-2 cloves garlic, finely chopped

1 tablespoon parsley, finely chopped
Salt and freshly ground pepper

1 In a mortar, combine slightly softened butter with finely chopped garlic and parsley and pound until it is well mixed. Add salt and freshly ground pepper, to taste. Mix well. Transfer butter to a roll of clingfilm. Roll into a small sausage shape and chill until ready to serve.

2 When ready to serve: Remove butter from refrigerator; unwrap clingfilm; trim ends and slice into 0.5cm/¼ inch rounds.

Oven Roasting

Roasting is essentially cooking meats, poultry or game in an oven or on a spit, without covering the food in stock or sauce. It's simple to do but timing is crucial.

Prime cuts of beef, veal, lamb or pork make successful roasts, but only the prime cuts. If you are ever in any doubt about the quality of a piece of meat, casserole it or pot-roast it instead.

A small joint (900g/2 lb or under) doesn't make a successful roast either, however good its quality. By the time the inevitable shrinkage has occurred, there will be little left. Again, settle for the more gentle pot-roasting or casseroling instead.

The cuts of beef suitable for roasting are the ribs, sirloin and fillet and, in best-quality beef, the rump. Suitable cuts of lamb are the leg, saddle, loin and shoulder. Pork roasts include the leg, loin and spare rib. The loin, saddle, leg, shoulder, rump, and often the breast of veal, can all be roasted.

Tips for Oven Roasting

1 Take meat out of the refrigerator sufficently ahead of roasting time to allow it to come to room temperature.
2 Roast beef in a hot oven, 200-220°C/400-425°F/Gas 6-7, for 15-30 minutes to seal it. Then reduce oven heat to 160-170°C/325°F/Gas 3, and continue to cook until done.
3 Baste meat frequently with pan juices whether it is cooked on the spit or in the oven, beginning about 30 minutes after the meat has started to cook. Baste every 10-15 minutes.
4 An oven roast should always be placed on a grid so that the meat does not come into contact with the juices and fat which have drained from it into the pan beneath.

To test roasts for doneness

Take a sharp, thin, metal skewer or a long fork with no more than two sharp prongs to it; push it into the thickest part of the meat (right through to the bone, if there is one) and pull it out again. You will be able to tell the state of the meat from the colour of the juices that spurt out. The test spot in poultry is right through the thickest part of the inside leg (i.e. where the leg lies close to the body).

One or two tests should be enough. Resist the temptation to jab your roast full of holes like a pin cushion.

Beef

I like to roast beef at a low temperature for an even texture. Roast beef in a fairly hot oven (200-220°C/400-425°F/Gas 6-7) for 15-30 minutes to seal it. Then reduce oven heat to 170°C/325°F/Gas 3 and continue to cook until done.

Veal

It is very important to roast veal slowly, too, so that it is still juicy with just a hint of firmness. Most cooks make the mistake of letting it go on to the stage of being stringy and dry. You'll be amazed at the difference if you try low-temperature roasting the next time you roast veal.

Lamb

Lamb should never be overcooked. It is at its best - moist and richly flavoured - when it is a little pink on the inside. I like to cook it for 20-25 minutes per 450g/1 lb at a relatively low temperature (150-170°C/300-325°F/Gas 2-3) for roasting, and a bare simmer for cooking in liquid.

Pork

Pork is best if roasted at about 150-170°F/300-325°F/Gas 2-3 with plenty of cooking time and basting to give the skin or crackling a nice flavour and texture. All cuts of tender, fairly fat pork can be roasted. Cook it until the meat has lost its pinkish tinge and is pale beige in colour. I like to roast pork in a slow to moderate oven (150-170°F/300-325°F/Gas 2-3) for about 35 minutes per 450g/1 lb.

Duck

There are two schools of thought on cooking duck. One widely held theory is that for maximum flavour and succulence duck should be roasted for 15-20 minutes per 450g/1 lb at a high temperature (230°C/450°F/Gas 8).

I find that cooking a duckling in a slow oven gives the best results, with a straight 180°C/350°F/Gas 4 temperature right through the cooking time.

Goose

Place goose, breast side down, on a rack in a shallow roasting pan. Prick fatty parts of the goose with a fork to help draw out remaining fat during cooking. Roast goose at 200°C/400°F/Gas 6 for 15 minutes, and then in a very slow oven (150°C/300°F/Gas 2) for 2 hours, pouring off fat during roasting as it accumulates. Then turn goose and cook for 1½-2 hours more, until goose is nicely browned and the meat is very tender. You will find that long, slow cooking at this temperature will cook out excess fat and leave meat juicy and tender.

Turkey

Roast stuffed turkey in a slow oven (170°C/325°F/Gas 3) for 3½-4 hours for a 4.5 - 5.4 kg/10-12 lb oven-ready bird, allowing about 15 minutes per extra 450g/1 lb for larger birds. To let turkey brown and crisp, remove bacon and muslin 20-30 minutes before turkey is done.

Roast Guinea Fowl with Aromatic Butter

SERVES 6

3 guinea fowl, poussins or partridges	*Juice of ½ lemon*
1 teaspoon crushed thyme	*Juice of 1 orange*
½ teaspoon rosemary leaves	*1 Spanish onion, chopped*
1 clove garlic	*3 tablespoons finely chopped parsley*
6 juniper berries	*Pinch of grated nutmeg or mace*
100g/4oz butter, diced	*Salt and freshly ground pepper*

1 To make aromatic butter: Combine crushed thyme, rosemary, garlic and juniper berries in a mortar and pound until well blended. Add diced butter and lemon and orange juice, alternately, pounding again until well blended.

2 Stir in chopped onion and parsley, a pinch of grated nutmeg or mace, and generous amounts of salt and freshly ground pepper. The mixture should be highly flavoured. Brush birds inside and out with this aromatic butter and allow meat to absorb flavours overnight.

3 To roast birds: Place in a heatproof roasting pan and cook in a preheated oven (220°C/425°F/Gas 7) for 25-35 minutes, basting frequently with melted aromatic butter. Birds are cooked when juices run quite clear when you insert a skewer through the thickest part of the leg.

French Roast Lemon Chicken

SERVES 4

1.8kg/4 lb free range chicken
100g/4 oz good butter
Salt and freshly ground pepper
Crushed dried chillies
1½ lemons
Several sprigs of thyme or tarragon,
  or a mixture of the two

Garnish
Fine Julienne of lemon zest
Sprigs of watercress or fresh herbs

1 To prepare the lemon butter for the chicken: In a small bowl, mash the butter with a wooden fork or spoon until creamy and add a good pinch of salt, freshly ground pepper and crushed dried chillies to taste.

2 Squeeze the juice of one lemon into the flavoured butter. Add the leaves of a few sprigs of thyme or tarragon, or a mixture of the two. Mix well and rub mixture all over the chicken.

3 Preheat the oven to 180°C/350°F/Gas 4.

4 Place the remaining half lemon inside the chicken. Place the chicken on a rack in a roasting pan and roast in the pre-heated oven for 55-65 minutes, basting the chicken with its buttery juices from time to time.

Basic Roast Chicken

SERVES 4

1 roasting chicken (1.6-1.8kg/ 3½-4 lb)	Watercress
Watercress stuffing	Lemon juice
2 slices fat bacon	Salt
Butter	300ml/½ pint chicken stock
1 tablespoon sifted flour	Freshly ground pepper

1 Loosen the skin at the neck end of a cleaned, trussed roasting chicken as much as possible from the breast. Insert stuffing over the flesh of the breast and fill the loose skin of the neck with as much as it will hold. Fold the skin over and fasten with 1 or 2 stitches. Stuff body cavity as well.

2 Tie 1 or 2 slices of fat bacon over the breast, making 1 or 2 slits in the bacon to prevent it from curling. Cover the bird with waxed paper and roast in a slow oven (170°C/325°F/Gas 3), basting frequently with butter, for 1-1½ hours, according to the size and age of the bird. Test it by feeling the flesh of the leg; if it gives way to pressure it is ready. A few minutes before the end of cooking time, remove the paper and bacon and sprinkle the breast lightly with flour. Baste well, turn up the oven temperature to 200°C/400°F/Gas 6 and brown quickly.

3 When ready to serve, put bird on a hot serving dish and remove the trussing string. Garnish with watercress seasoned with lemon juice and salt. Pour away the fat from the roasting pan, add chicken stock and stir over a high heat until boiling, scraping in any brown bits from sides of pan. Season to taste with salt and freshly ground pepper, and serve in a sauceboat.

Watercress Stuffing

6 tablespoons onion, finely chopped	Lemon juice
6 tablespoons celery, finely chopped	Salt and freshly ground pepper
6 tablespoons butter	½lb fresh breadcrumbs, slightly toasted
1 bunch watercress, finely chopped	in oven

1 Simmer the finely chopped onion and celery in ½ the butter until soft. Add finely chopped watercress and season with lemon juice, salt and freshly ground pepper, to taste. Continue cooking until all liquids eveporate. Melt the remaining butter. Stir in the breadcrumbs and then add to the watercress mixture. Stuff the chicken with this mixture and roast as above.

Roast Rolled Topside of Beef

SERVES 4

1.1- 1.4kg/ 2½-3lb topside of beef
4 tablespoons dripping or butter
1 tablespoon dry mustard
Coarsely ground pepper

2 tablespoon slightly browned flour
4 tablespoons warm water or red wine
Salt

1 At least 2 hours before you intend to roast beef, remove joint from the refrigerator. Preheat oven to 220°C/ 425°F/Gas 7.

2 Spread beef generously with dripping or butter and sprinkle with a mixture of dry mustard, coarsely ground pepper and flour (which you have lightly browned in a frying pan or in the oven).

3 Place beef on a rack over a roasting pan and brown in the oven for 20 minutes. Lower heat to 170°C/325°F/Gas 3. Add warm water or red wine and continue to roast, basting occasionally, until beef is done to your liking (a further 15 minutes per pound for rare, and 20 minutes per pound for medium) adding a little more wine or water as necessary.

4 When the beef is cooked, remove it from the oven and place it on a well-heated serving platter. Leave it to stand in a warm place for 10-15 minutes 'to settle'.

5 Season beef with salt and additional freshly ground pepper just before serving.

Roast Rolled Topside of Beef

Roast Saddle of Lamb

Roast Saddle of Lamb

SERVES 6-8

1 saddle of lamb (about 3.2kg/ 7lb)
Softened butter
Salt and freshly ground pepper
Crushed rosemary
425ml/ ¾ pint beef stock
1 tablespoon butter
1 tablespoon plain flour
Sprigs of watercress

Aromatics:
½ Spanish onion, finely chopped
8 sprigs fresh thyme
8 cloves garlic, blackened

1 Preheat the oven to 190°C/ 375°F/ Gas 5.

2 Spread the lamb with softened butter and sprinkle with salt, freshly ground pepper and crushed rosemary.

3 Place the saddle in a roasting pan; pour 150ml/¼pint water around it; place it in the preheated oven and roast for 1 hour, basting frequently.

4 Remove the roast from the oven. Skim off the fat from the pan; add the beef stock and a *beurre manie* (made from 1 tablespoon butter mixed to a smooth paste with 1 tablespoon of flour) and cook over a high heat, stirring in all the crusty bits from the sides of the pan, until the sauce is smooth and thick. Strain and keep warm.

5 Place the partially roasted saddle of lamb in an oiled roasting pan in which you have scattered finely chopped onion, sprigs of fresh thyme, garlic cloves and salt and freshly ground pepper, to taste. Roast for another 30-45 minutes (15 minutes per pound in all) or until the lamb is tender.

6 Place the lamb on a large heated serving dish and garnish with the aromatics and sprigs of fresh watercress. Serve the sauce separately.

Roast Loin of Pork

SERVES 4-6

1 loin of pork (4-6 chops), chined
6 tablespoons softened butter
1 ½ tablespoons French
  mustard
2 bay leaves, crumbled

½ teaspoon dried rosemary
  or thyme
Salt and freshly ground pepper
3-4 sage leaves, quartered
12-16 slivers of garlic

1 Preheat oven to hot (230°C/450°F/Gas 8).

2 With the point of a sharp knife, make 12-16 incisions all over the joint about 2.5cm/1 inch deep.

3 Blend butter with French mustard, crumbled bay leaves and rosemary or thyme.

4 Season pork with salt and freshly ground pepper and spread with mustard butter, making sure it goes deep into the incisions.

5 Stick a quartered sage leaf and a sliver of garlic into each incision with the point of a sharp knife.

6 Roast in the usual way, lowering the heat to 150°C/300°F/Gas 2 after the first 15 minutes. Serve with tomato halves scooped out and filled with sliced mushrooms, which have been sautéed in butter.

Frying

Frying is simply the cooking of food in very hot fat or oil. The term is also extended to pan-frying (or sautéing) and in America many foods are oven-fried, a combination of sautéing and baking which has much to recommend it for simple dishes.

Pan-frying

Pan-frying is to fry food gently in a very little hot fat or oil, shaking the pan or turning the food being fried frequently during cooking. For best results pan-fry tender meats, fish or vegetables. Avoid overloading the pan or covering it during cooking as this removes the crispness of the food and makes the food soggy.

I have three favourite kinds of pans for pan-frying in my kitchen: 1) An old-fashioned black iron frying pan with a thick, heavy bottom so that it stands steady on the stove top and conducts heat evenly all across the surface of the pan. I use this pan for great breakfast fry-ups of rashers and bacon and eggs. 2) A non-stick black-finished frying pan in three handy sizes (25cm/ 9½ inch, 28cm/11½ inch and 33cm/ 13 inch) with stainless steel handles absolutely guaranteed not to get hot while in use. I use the smallest pan (just brushed with oil) to sear fresh scallops and red snapper before popping the pan in a preheated oven to continue cooking the fish for another 3-5 minutes. I use the two larger pans for potato and cheese *galettes*, *frittatas* and *tortillas* and for pan-fried vegetables. 3) My newly acquired stainless steel frying pans and saute pans (again with patented 'stay cool' handles) from Brazil.

Saute pans are different from fry pans in that they have higher sides and are specially made so that small pieces of meat, fish and poultry can be tosssed over a high heat during the cooking (sauteeing) process. Saute literally means 'jump' and as you shake the pan over the heat , the food 'jumps' about in the pan, protected by the pan's high sides. In this way, the food sticking to the bottom of the saute pan is dislodged and the new surfaces are constantly being exposed to the heat.

Oven Frying

A way of frying much used in America is oven frying. The foods to be oven fried are tossed in hot fat and then placed in an ovenproof dish in a preheated oven to continue cooking until they are cooked through and golden brown. Oven frying is simpler to execute than pan-frying as there is no need to shake the pan or worry about charring the foods; the even flow of oven heat ensures that all parts of the foods being oven fried are cooked through equally.

Fragile fish such as lemon sole or plaice are particularly good for cooking in this manner as there is no danger of the fish 'breaking up' during pan-frying or sautéeing. To make a delicious version of *plaice à la niçoise*, just dip the fish in a little milk and then breadcrumbs (already mixed with equal quantities of finely chopped parsley and garlic, grated lemon peel and ¼ teaspoon rubbed thyme). Arrange the fish in a buttered baking dish and pour over 4-6 tablespoons melted butter. Place the dish on the top shelf of a preheated oven (200°C/400°F/ Gas 6) for about 12 minutes.

Quick Pan-fried Vegetables

Quick Pan-fried Vegetables

SERVES 4

450g/1lb vegetables of your choice
(see list below)
Olive oil

¼ vegetable stock cube
1 pinch crushed dried chillies
Sea salt and freshly ground pepper

1 Wash the vegetables and slice diagonally across the grain. If using broccoli or cauliflower, break (or cut) off florets.

2 Blanch sliced vegetables by cooking in boiling salted water (see times below), and drain.

Carrots	5-6 minutes
Courgettes	2-3 minutes
Broccoli	3 minutes
Cauliflower	3 minutes
Green beans	3 minutes
Asparagus	2-3 minutes
Celery	2 minutes
Sugar snap peas	2 minutes
Mangetout	2 minutes

3 In a large stainless steel sauté pan or black non-stick frying pan, sauté blanched vegetables in 2 tablespoons of oil for 1-2 minutes. Add ½ crumbled vegetable stock cube, a pinch of crushed dried chillies, salt and freshly ground pepper to taste, and cook for 2-3 minutes longer. Serve immediately.

Sauté d'Agneau aux Flageolets

SERVES 4

2 best ends (racks) of lamb, trimmed
Freshly ground pepper
1 bay leaf
Olive oil
225g/7½ oz can flageolets
Salt
Butter

Garnish
225g/8 oz okra or green beans,
   blanched (as above) and sautéed
   in a little butter
2 tablespoons finely chopped parsley or
chives

Sauce
Bones and trimmings from lamb
½ chicken stock cube
2 tablespoons tomato purée
½ Spanish onion, finely chopped
1 bay leaf
4 tablespoons dry white wine
Beurre manie: Made by mashing together
   1 tablespoon each butter and flour to a
   smooth paste
Salt and freshly ground pepper

1 Cut meat from the bones of best ends (or racks) of lamb, making a 'fillet'. Cut the 'fillet' into 2.5cm/1 inch thick slices. Trim each slice into 3 or 4 even-sized cubes, according to size of lamb. Reserve bones, meat trimmings and scraps for sauce.

2 Season lamb cubes generously with freshly ground pepper and place in an ovenware or porcelain bowl (not metal). Add bay leaf and 4 tablespoons olive oil and toss well. Leave lamb to marinate for at least 2 hours.

3 To make sauce: Chop reserved lamb bones coarsely and place in a thick-bottomed saucepan with meat trimmings, scraps, chicken stock cube, tomato purée, onion, bay leaf and wine. Add enough water to just cover and simmer gently until meat on bones is cooked through.

4 Strain stock into clean pan and cook over a high heat until reduced to half its original quantity. Whisk in *beurre manie*eSeason with freshly ground pepper and salt, if necessary. Keep warm.

5 Drain flageolets, season with salt and freshly ground pepper and sauté for a few minutes in a little butter. Keep warm.

6 In a large frying pan, sear lamb in marinating oil until golden brown on all sides but still quite rare. Pour off excess fats.

7 Add sauce to pan and bring to the bubble. Garnish with hot flageolets and okra or green beans. Sprinkle with finely chopped parsley or chives. Serve immediately.

Pan-Fried Veal with Lemon

SERVES 4

450g/1 lb boneless veal, loin or fillet
Salt and freshly ground pepper
1 tablespoon olive oil
4 tablespoons butter
8 paper-thin slices lemon

4 spring onions, sliced thinly
1 sprig fresh tarragon or rosemary
2 tablespoons finely chopped parsley
4 tablespoons dry white wine (optional)

1 Slice veal into 8-16 pieces according to the size and pound slices flat. Season veal on both sides with salt and freshly ground pepper.

2 Heat olive oil and 2 tablespoons butter in a frying pan. When foaming, add veal, lemon slices, spring onions and herbs and cook veal for 1 minute on each side, or until cooked through but still juicy.

3 Transfer veal and lemon slices to a heated dish with a slotted spoon. Keep warm. Add remaining butter to the pan, together with a little dry white wine (or water) and heat gently, scraping surface of the pan clean with a wooden spoon. Pour pan juices over hot veal and lemon and serve immediately.

Calf's Liver with Sage and Avocado

SERVES 4

2 avocado pears
Lemon juice
8 thin slices calf's liver
Flour
Salt and freshly ground pepper

4 tablespoons butter
1 tablespoon olive oil
6 sage leaves
6 tablespoons reduced veal or beef stock

1 Peel avocados, remove stones and slice thinly. Brush each slice with a little lemon juice to preserve colour.

2 Dip liver slices in flour, well seasoned with salt and freshly ground pepper.

3 Melt butter and olive oil in a frying pan, add sage leaves and sauté calf's liver very quickly on both sides. Add reduced veal or beef stock and a squeeze of lemon juice to pan. Top liver slices with sliced avocado. Warm through and serve immediately.

Stir Frying

Stir frying is probably the most characteristic method of Chinese cooking - and it is the most versatile. Practically anything that can be cooked can be stir-fried. You will find that stir frying is easy too once you have learned to judge the proper degree of heat and the proper method of cutting the ingredients to be stir-fried. And, what is even more important, the proper order of putting the ingredients into your wok, or other cooking utensil.

Moistness and tenderness are all important in this method of cooking. I like to use fillet of beef or veal, fillet or spare ribs of pork and breast of chicken, duck or pigeon. And remember, it is absolutely essential to prepare all your ingredients before you actually start cooking because ingredients (mostly vegetables, meats and seasonings) are put into the wok literally seconds apart. There will be no time for slicing and cutting extra ingredients when you need them. Before cooking, I like to set out the sliced or cubed vegetables, meat and other ingredients in separate little dishes within easy reach of the wok and in the order in which they are to be used.

The preparation of the foods to be stir-fried is most important because it determines the final appearance of the dish as well as the length of time the food is to be cooked. Make sure all foods are cut into the same size for the same dish. You will find that food cut into small pieces - whether diced, cubed or cut into strips - cooks quickly and is easy to season. When meats and vegetables are combined in one dish, as is often the way in Chinese stir frying, they are actually cooked separately. Vegetables are usually cooked first, removed from the wok and then the meats cooked. At the last minute, they are both returned to the wok for a final heating through and seasoning before being served. And remember, Chinese food must be served very hot. Right from the wok for the best results. So, happy cooking.

Chinese Beef with Oyster Sauce

SERVES 2

350g/12 oz rump or sirloin steak	**Marinade**
1 green pepper, stem and seeds removed	4 tablespoons fermented black beans*
1 red pepper, stem and seeds removed	3 tablespoons oyster sauce*
Vegetable oil	½ teaspoon Chinese chilli (hot pepper) sauce*
Finely chopped ginger	2 tablespoons soy sauce
Finely chopped garlic	4 tablespoons dry white wine
	2 tablespoons vegetable oil
	Strips of spring onion, sliced lengthwise, to garnish

1 Trim steak of fat and cut the meat diagonally into thin strips. Place the strips in a shallow bowl.

2 Cut the peppers into thin strips and place them in a separate bowl.

3 Combine the marinade ingredients and pour half over the meat and half over the peppers.

4 Brush the wok with a few drops of oil and heat over a high heat.

5 Add 1 teaspoon each finely chopped ginger and garlic to wok, gently stirring to keep from browning.

6 Add the marinated pepper strips and cook, stirring, for 1 minute.

7 With a slotted spoon, transfer pepper strips to a plate, add the beef strips to the wok and cook, stirring constantly, until beef is browned on all sides.

8 Return peppers to wok and continue to cook, stirring, for 1-2 minutes more or until beef is cooked.

9 Add the spring onion strips and stir to heat through. Serve immediately.

* Available from some supermarkets and Chinese food stores.

Stir-fried Prawns with Broccoli

SERVES 2

225g/8 oz cooked, shelled prawns
100g/4 oz broccoli florets
1 tablespoon cornflour
1-2 tablespoons dry white wine
2 tablespoons sake* or dry sherry
2 tablespoons tomato purée
1 teaspoon sugar
Dash of Chinese chilli (hot pepper) sauce*

2 tablespoons soy sauce
1-1½ teaspoons sesame oil*
6 tablespoons peanut oil
1½ teaspoons finely shredded root ginger
1-1½ teaspoons finely shredded garlic
1-1½ tablespoons thinly sliced spring onion

1 Divide the broccoli into small florets. Blanch them in boiling water for 1 minute, then drain well.

2 Place the prawns in a large shallow dish. Blend the cornflour with the dry white wine. Pour over the prawns and stir well.

3 Combine the sake or sherry, tomato purée, sugar, chilli sauce, soy sauce, sesame oil and 4 tablespoons peanut oil in a small bowl.

4 In a wok heated with remaining oil, add the prawns in their marinade and cook for 30 seconds.

5 Add the ginger, garlic and spring onion to the wok and stir fry for 1 minute.

6 Add the soy mixture and stir fry for 1 minute.

7 Add the broccoli florets and toss for 1 minute. Serve immediately.

* Available from some supermarkets and Chinese food stores.

Quick Sautéed Cherry Tomatoes

450g/1lb cherry tomatoes
2-3 tablespoons olive oil
Pinch or two of sea salt

Pinch crushed dried chillies
4-6 spring onions finely sliced, or cut into
5-7cm/2-3 inch segments

1 Heat the oil in a large frying pan.

2 Add the cherry tomatoes and sauté over a fairly high heat until skins begin to split.

3 Add the sea salt, crushed dried chillies and spring onions and heat through. Serve as a colourful accompaniment to roasts, e.g. chicken, beef, pork.

Deep-frying

The way you fry is more important than the fat or oil you use. The less oil or fat absorbed during frying, the better the quality of the fried food. Deep-fried food should never be greasy so the fat must be hot enough to 'carbonize' the exterior of what is being fried at the very moment of immersion. This prevents grease from penetrating the food, conserves the juices, and allows the food to retain all its taste. Deep-frying is simple and quick when you know how.

Vegetable fats and vegetable oils are good for all deep-frying. Rendered beef fat is a good choice for meats, fish croquettes and less delicate foods. Chicken fat and butter are not suitable for deep-frying because they scorch at low temperatures. Whatever oil or fat you use, it should be fresh and of good quality.

A frying medium uses itself up quickly, especially when it is heated to excess. I have found I can double the life of my frying oil if I never allow it to smoke or boil. Use the bread test instead: drop 2.5cm/1 inch cube of day-old bread in the hot oil. If your temperature is right for deep-frying (190°C/375°F) the bread should brown in about 60 seconds.

1 Do not allow fat to smoke or boil.

2 The temperature of the fat should vary as little as possible during cooking.

3 If you plunge food into the fat a second time, the temperature of the second cooking must be higher than that of the first.

To deep-fry fish

When properly fried, fish should be a light golden brown, dry and crisp in texture, and completely free of fat. I like to deep-fry fish in a light vegetable oil, or at other times, a combination of lard and oil to give added flavour

Small fish are better fried whole, large ones should be filleted or cut into steaks or cutlets.

To fry well, fish should be perfectly dry. Always pat fish dry with a clean cloth or paper towel before coating with seasoned flour, fine oatmeal or cornmeal, beaten egg and dry breadcrumbs, or a frying batter. This prevents fat from entering the fish while it is immersed in the hot cooking fat or oil and adds a flavoursome, crunchy coating to complement the delicately flavoured flesh within.

If seasoned flour or flour and milk are used as a coating, apply just before the fish is to be cooked, or the flour will become moist and the fish will not fry well. Batter, too, should be applied only at the last moment.

Deep-Fried 'Fish-n-Chips'

SERVES 4–6

675g/1½lb cod or halibut fillet
6 tablespoons lemon juice
½ Spanish onion, finely chopped
Salt and cayenne pepper
6 medium-sized potatoes
Oil for deep frying

Aromatic flavouring for fish
100g/4 oz sifted flour
1 teaspoon paprika
1 teaspoon salt
Cayenne pepper
2 lemons, cut into wedges
Light beer batter (see page 122)
Home-made tomato chutney (see page 122)

1 Cut fish into serving pieces, 2 or 3 pieces per serving.

2 Place fish in a flat porcelain bowl and sprinkle with lemon juice, finely chopped onion and salt and cayenne pepper, to taste. Allow fish to marinate in this mixture for 1 hour.

3 To make 'chips': wash and peel the potatoes, cutting them into fat strips about 7.5cm/3 inches long. Rinse in cold water and drain thoroughly.

4 Heat oil to 190°C/375°F. Fill frying basket one-half to two-thirds full of potatoes and immerse it gently into the hot oil. Shake the basket from time to time while frying to keep potatoes from sticking together. Continue to fry until potatoes are nearly tender. Drain well and spread on a pan lined with paper towels to absorb excess oil while you fry remaining potatoes.

5 To make aromatic flavouring for fish. Sift flour, paprika, salt, and freshly ground pepper and cayenne pepper to taste, on to a flat dish. Dust the fish thoroughly in the seasoned mix.

6 Or, make light beer batter (see page 122) and dip fish, piece-by-piece into the batter.

7 Deep fry fish in the same oil (make sure heat is 190°C/375°F) until golden brown and crisp. Place fish in a pan lined with paper towels and keep warm.

8 Bring oil to 190°C/375°F again, and refry potatoes in small quantities in frying basket until golden brown. Drain.

9 Serve fish and chips together in a heated serving dish. Garnish with lemon wedges, and serve with a bowl of home-made tomato chutney.

Home-made Tomato Chutney

*5lb ripe tomatoes, quartered
  and seeded
450g/1lb Spanish onions, sliced
450g/1lb cooking apples,
  peeled, cored and sliced
450g/1lb demerara sugar
1 teaspoon salt*

*1 teaspoon allspice
½ teaspoon mustard seed
150ml/¼ pint water
Malt vinegar
½ teaspoon cayenne pepper
1 short cinnamon stick
6 cloves*

1 In a large enamelled pan (or preserving pan) combine the tomatoes, onions, apples, sugar, salt, allspice and mustard seed and cook, stirring from time to time, to keep the ingredients from sticking to the bottom of the pan. Add ¼ pint water and malt vinegar,to taste, plus cayenne pepper and cloves; stir well and simmer for 2–2½ hours, stirring occasionally. Make sure that the pan is almost coveredwith a large china dish (not a metal lid) to keep the juices form evaporating.

2 While the chutney is still hot, pour it into sterilized, dry, warm preserving jars. Place a piece of greasproof paper over the chutney in each jar before you seal it. Store in a dry place.

Light Beer Batter

MAKES 300ml/ ½ PINT

*125g/5 oz plain flour
2Pinches of salt
2 tablespoons olive oil*

*150ml/¼ pint beer, preferably lager
2-4 tablespoons water
1 egg white*

1 Sift flour and salt into a bowl, and make a well in the centre.

2 Pour in olive oil and gradually add beer, stirring with a wooden spoon to incorporate flour from sides of well. Batter should be completely smooth and slightly thicker than a crepe batter. Add water if needed. Leave to rest for 2 hours.

3 When ready to use batter: whisk egg white until stiff but not dry, and fold in gently but thoroughly. Use immediately as a light batter for meat, poultry, vegetables, fish and shellfish.

Deep-fried Aubergines and Courgettes

SERVES 4-6

2 aubergines
4 courgettes
Oil, for deep frying
Flour

2-3 eggs, lightly beaten
Fine breadcrumbs
Salt and freshly ground pepper
Cayenne pepper

1 Do not peel aubergines or courgettes. Cut aubergines crossways into 0.5cm/¼ inch slices, then cut each slice into strips 0.5cm/¼-inch thick. Trim ends from courgettes and cut each across into 2 equal-sized pieces. Cut each piece in 2 lengthways and remove seeds. Then cut into 0.5cm/¼ inch thick strips.

2 Preheat oven to 140°C/275°F/Gas 1.

3 Half-fill the deep-fryer with oil and heat it to 190°C/375°F.

4 Dip aubergine and courgettes strips, a few at a time, into flour, then into lightly beaten eggs and then into breadcrumbs. Fry strips, 12-20 at a time, in hot oil until golden brown.

5 To keep vegetables hot: As vegetable strips are fried, lift them from frying basket and let them drain for a minute or two on a baking sheet lined with paper kitchen towels. Keep warm in preheated oven.

6 Season generously with salt, freshly ground pepper and cayenne and serve at once.

Cooking in a Casserole

Casseroling food involves cooking it on a slow gentle heat, either on top of a stove or in a moderate oven. Casserole ingredients can be meat, vegetables or a mix of both, and the food is cooked until tender in a well-flavoured stock with a seasoning. Your casserole dish should be able to withstand long hours of heat and, for best results, should be kept covered with a tight fitting lid throughout cooking .

Casseroling is simply a combination of roasting, stewing and steaming. The meat to be braised is sometimes (Step 1) larded; often (Step 2) marinated; always (Step 3) browned in fat and then (Step 4) cooked gently, covered, in a little liquid to preserve juices and flavour. In the classic French method, the casserole is lined with a layer of diced or sliced vegetables before slow simmering begins.

Generally, meat, poultry or fish to be braised is braised in the piece. However, the braising techniques listed below can also be used with great facility for cut-up pieces of meat, poultry or fish in stews, ragoûts, daubes and casseroles.

Larding

Top-quality beef (rib or fillet) does not need larding, but it is usually wise to lard rump or round of beef, a roast of veal or a leg of mutton with strips of bacon fat as long as the piece of meat to be cooked and about 1 cm/½ inch wide. Season these first with freshly ground black pepper and spices, sprinkle with chopped parsley and marinate for about 2 hours in a little brandy; then insert the strips into the meat with a special larding needle. Most butchers will lard meat for you.

Marinating

The flavour of meat intended for braising is greatly improved by marinating it for a few hours in the wine which is to be the moistening agent in cooking. Roll the meat in a mixture of salt, freshly ground black pepper and finely chopped herbs, and place it in an earthenware casserole just large enough to hold it, on a bed of thickly sliced carrots and onions, a generous bouquet garni, a clove or two of garlic, and some blanched, fried fat bacon. Cover the meat with wine and marinate for at least 2 hours in this mixture, taking care to turn it several times during this period.

Sautéeing

After marinating the meat, drain it well and wipe dry with a clean cloth. Sauté in a little olive oil, bacon fat, butter or lard, or a combination of these, to colour it and seal in its juices. Then place the vegetables and herbs from the marinade in the bottom of a heavy casserole or braising pan just large enough to hold the meat. Place the meat on this bed of aromatics and pour in enough of the juices from the marinade to cover the vegetables generously.

Casserole of Duck with Red Wine

Casseroling

Add well-flavoured beef stock and bring it to the boil. Cover the casserole and cook gently on top of the stove or in a moderate oven (120°C/250°F/Gas ½) until the meat can be pricked deeply with a fork without releasing blood. Remove the meat to another casserole just large enough to hold it, strain the sauce over meat through a piece of muslin and place casserole, covered, in the oven. Cook until meat is tender, basting from time to time to keep the top moist. Before serving, correct seasoning and thicken the sauce, if necessary, with *beurre manie* (equal quantities of flour and butter mixed together).

Cook very slowly so that the meat is tender and the fat rises gradually to the surface of the liquid.

Vegetables can also be braised this way with excellent results.

Years ago, in a book called *The Robert Carrier Cookery Course*, now sadly out of print, I wrote about the major thickeners used to 'finish' a casserole before bringing it to the table. I repeat these valuable instructions here.

To Finish a Casserole

When your casserole is cooked, your sauce may need thickening. If this is to involve simmering or boiling, lift the meat out first with a slotted spoon and keep it hot in a covered bowl. Next, skim the surface of fat, if necessary, either drawing a spoon over the surface, or by 'dusting' it with sheets of absorbent kitchen paper until all the fat has been removed. To thicken the sauce, use one of the following methods:

Reduction: The simplest way, provided the casserole has not been too highly seasoned and already has some thickening - either 'melted' vegetables or a dusting of flour before the meat was sauteed - is to boil the sauce briskly, stirring constantly to stimulate evaporation, until it has reduced to the desired consistency. It can then be rubbed through a fine sieve or left as it is.

Beurre Manie: This is made by combining equal volumes (not weights) of butter and flour in a small bowl or cup, and mashing them to a smooth paste. Take up tiny pieces of this paste on the tip of your spoon and stir them into the simmering sauce. Because of its high butter content, the paste will have no difficulty dissolving without giving the flour a chance to form lumps. Bring to the boil and simmer for 3-4 minutes to ensure flour is cooked and no longer tastes raw.

Flour or Cornflour: Worked smoothly with water and stirred briskly into the simmering sauce (to prevent lumps forming) is a quick, if crude way, of thickening and one that I do not particularly like. Flour on its own tends to make a sauce unnecessarily heavy and cornflour, while lighter and eminently suitable for some sauces, especially sweet ones, or Chinese ones, gives a characteristic 'super-glossy' texture which seems out of place in a robust casserole of meat, poultry or game.

Casserole of Duck with Red Wine

SERVES 4-6

1 tender duck (2-3kg / 5-6 lb,
   or 2 smaller ones)
2 stalks celery, sliced
2 carrots, sliced
2 large onions, sliced
4 tablespoons Cognac
450ml/¾ pint dry red wine
Salt and freshly ground pepper

100g /4 oz bacon, diced
4 tablespoons olive oil
2 tablespoons dry sherry
1 tablespoon wine vinegar
2 tablespoons butter
1 tablespoon flour
Bouquet garni
2 cloves garlic

1 Cut duck into serving pieces and place in a porcelain or earthenware bowl. Add sliced celery, carrots and onions, Cognac and red wine and season with salt and freshly ground pepper, to taste. Marinate the duck in this mixture overnight.

2 Remove duck pieces from the marinade. Drain and pat dry, reserving marinade.

3 Saute diced bacon in olive oil in a heatproof casserole, until golden. Remove bacon dice and reserve. Add duck pieces and cook over a medium heat in remaining fat until brown on all sides. Return bacon to casserole; cover and simmer duck and bacon pieces gently for 20 minutes. Skim excess fat from pan juices. Add sherry and wine vinegar and stir over high heat for 2-3 minutes. Remove from heat and keep warm.

4 To prepare sauce: While duck is cooking, make a roux with butter and flour. In a small, heavy saucepan, melt the butter over a low heat until it is frothy, but not coloured. Add the flour and stir with a wooden spoon until the two are smoothly combined. Continue to simmer the mixture, stirring constantly and reaching into the corners of the pan until the roux turns a rich golden brown colour.

5 Strain the hot marinade juices into roux mixture and stir over a low heat, until smooth andthick. Add marinade vegetables, bouquet garni and garlic to the thickened sauce and simmer over a very low heat for 20 minutes.

6 To finish casserole: Remove bouquet garni from sauce and skim off excess fat. Strain sauce through a fine sieve over duck and bacon in casserole, pressing vegetables well to extract full flavour. Continue to simmer duck pieces in sauce until tender. Serve with boiled noodles.

Chicken with 40 Cloves of Garlic (Poulet à l'Ail)

SERVES 4

1.4kg/3 lb chicken
Salt and freshly ground pepper
40 plump whole garlic cloves
3 tablespoons olive oil
3 tablespoons butter

4 fat leeks, white part only, thinly sliced
1 bay leaf
6-8 tablespoons dry white wine
6-8 tablespoons chicken stock

1 Preheat the oven to 110°C/225°F/Gas¼. Wipe the chicken clean with a damp cloth and season inside and out with salt and freshly ground pepper.

2 Remove the papery skins from the garlic cloves, but leave them whole. Put the garlic cloves in a small pan, cover with cold water and bring to boiling point. Drain thoroughly.

3 Choose a heavy, heatproof casserole just large enough to hold the chicken comfortably, and equipped with a tight-fitting lid. In it, heat 2 tablespoons each olive oil and butter, add the blanched garlic cloves and sauté for 3 - 4 minutes, stirring frequently. Take great care not to let the garlic cloves brown, or they will impart an unpleasantly bitter flavour to the dish. Remove the garlic cloves from the casserole with a slotted spoon and reserve.

4 Add the thinly sliced leeks to the casserole and sauté gently until the slices are soft and a rich golden colour. Remove with a slotted spoon and put aside with the garlic cloves. Then add the remaining oil and butter to the casserole. Raise the heat and brown the chicken steadily and thoroughly on all sides (approximately 10 minutes).

5 Return the sautéed garlic cloves and leeks to the casserole, season to taste with salt and freshly ground pepper; add the bay leaf. Add the white wine and chicken stock to the casserole. Cover the casserole tightly and transfer to the oven.

6 Cook for 1¼ hours, or until the chicken juices run clear when the leg is pierced through the thickest part close to the body, and the leeks have disintegrated to make a sauce.

7 Remove the chicken from the casserole and place on a heated serving dish. Remove the trussing string. Garnish with the garlic cloves. Spoon some of the pan juices over the chicken and serve the remainder in a heated sauce boat.

Ragoût of Lamb Provençale

SERVES 4-6

1.4kg/3 lb young lamb taken from
 shoulder and leg
Salt and freshly ground pepper
5 tablespoons butter

Marinade
2 Spanish onions, finely chopped
6 carrots, finely chopped
3 tablespoons olive oil
450ml/¾ pint dry white wine

Stock
Bones and trimmings from lamb
3 tablespoons olive oil
Marinade vegetables
1 tablespoon flour
2-3 tablespoons tomato purée
2 cloves garlic, mashed
300ml/½ pint well-flavoured stock

2 leeks, white parts only
2 stalks celery
4 sprigs parsley
1 bay leaf
1 sprig thyme
1 sprig rosemary
4 sage leaves
Butter

Garnish
24 black olives
4 carrots, peeled, sliced and simmered in
 butter with 2 strips orange peel
12 button onions, simmered in butter and
 lemon until tender
12 button mushrooms, simmered in butter
 and stock until tender
1 tablespoon finely chopped tarragon
1 tablespoon finely chopped parsley

1 Cut lamb into 3.5cm/1½inch cubes and season generously with salt and freshly ground pepper, rubbing seasoning well into meat with your fingers. Reserve bones and trimmings for stock.

2 Combine meat in a porcelain bowl with marinade ingredients and marinate in this mixture, turning from time to time, for at least 8 hours.

3 Drain meat (reserving marinade juices and vegetables) and season again with salt and freshly ground pepper.

4 To make stock: Place bones and trimmings in a baking tin. Moisten with olive oil and brown in a hot oven, turning the bones from time to time. Place bones and pan juices in a large heatproof casserole with marinade vegetables and cook over a high heat, stirring constantly, until vegetables are browned. Dust with flour and continue to cook for 5 more minutes. Add tomato purée, mashed garlic, stock, leeks, celery, parsley, bay leaf, thyme, rosemary and sage. Simmer gently for 1½ hours, adding a little more liquid if necessary. Strain stock through a fine sieve into a bowl and allow to cool. When cold, remove fat, dot with butter and reserve.

5 To cook lamb: Heat 3 tablespoons butter in a heatproof, thick-bottomed casserole until it sizzles. Place lamb cubes in casserole and sauté over a reasonably high heat until golden on all sides. Cover casserole and transfer to a preheated oven (180°C/350°F/Gas 4) and simmer gently for 1 hour, or until lamb is almost tender. Transfer lamb to a clean casserole and keep warm in a low oven.

6 Add prepared stock to casserole in which you have cooked lamb cubes and cook over a high heat, stirring in all the crusty bits from the sides of the pan, until sauce is reduced to half the original quantity. Add remaining butter, diced, and whisk until sauce is smooth. Correct seasoning and pour over lamb. Bring to the boil, reduce heat and simmer gently for 30-40 minutes, or until tender. Serve immediately, garnished with black olives, carrots, button onions and mushrooms, and sprinkled with finely chopped tarragon and parsley.

Osso Bucco

SERVES 4

4 thick slices shin of veal	*150ml/¼ pint boiling water or light stock*
Flour	*150ml/¼ pint dry white wine*
Salt and freshly ground pepper	*4 tablespoons tomato purée*
2 tablespoons olive oil	*4 anchovy fillets, finely chopped*
2 tablespoons butter	*4 tablespoons chopped parsley*
2 cloves garlic, finely chopped	*Grated rind of ½ lemon or orange*
½ Spanish onion, finely chopped	

1 Choose shin of veal with plenty of meat and have it sawn into pieces 5cm/2 inches thick.

2 Dredge veal pieces with flour, season with salt and freshly ground pepper, and brown them in olive oil and butter. Add half the finely chopped garlic and the onion and pour over boiling water or light stock, wine and tomato purée. Cover the pan and simmer gently over a very low heat for 1½ hours.

3 Add finely chopped anchovy fillets and remaining finely chopped garlic. Blend thoroughly, heat through and serve sprinkled with chopped parsley and grated lemon or orange rind, and accompanied by Risotto Milanese or saffron rice (see page 170).

Portuguese Pot Roast

Pot Roasting

Pot roasting is the general term for a cooking process that is as old as the first pot and the first fire. It is a natural way of cooking that gets the absolute maximum flavour and tenderness out of the more inexpensive cuts of meat. Pot roasting is really dry, or almost dry, casseroling, in which the meat and vegetables are first marinated in a rich wine marinade, 'roasted' in a very little fat in a heatproof casserole or iron pot called a Dutch oven and then simmered gently in the reduced juices of the marinade. This relatively small amount of liquid is the secret of successful pot roasting, making sure that the meat, poultry or game cooks very gently so that the flesh will be meltingly tender and the fat will rise gradually to the surface of the liquid so that it can be skimmed off.

Beef, particularly the top part of the shin, the rump, the topside, the brisket or the flank lends itself admirably to being pot roasted. Veal shoulder, breast, knuckle and shin make wonderful pot roasts too. Poultry, pot roasted with wine and well-flavoured stock, is a classic dish – or rather a host of classic dishes according to the part of the world we are considering. One of the most celebrated is Pot Roasted Duck with Turnips, a speciality of French provincial cooking that combines the duck with a full-bodied white wine, aromatics and tender young turnips. Cooked with care and attention, it is a model of pot roasting techniques.

I find that all pot roasts respond wonderfully well to this low-heat, one-pot cooking. Over the years I have gradually reduced the temperature at which I like to cook pot roasts (or daubes or casseroles), to 110°C/ 225°F/ Gas ¼ or 120°C/250°F/Gas ½. If I am cooking the pot roast on top of the stove, I like to use a wire mat to help keep the cooking down to a faint, barely perceptible simmer. Remember, this low oven temperature is not hot enough to bring the ingredients of a cold casserole up to simmering point. So, before you put the casserole or Dutch oven containing your pot roast into the oven, make sure you first bring the sauces gently to the bubble on top of the stove.

Pot roasting is easy. To start the process, brown the meat, poultry or vegetables in a little fat or oil to produce a coagulated, tasty residue that contributes considerably to the flavour, body and colour of the cooking liquids. Next the meat is removed and the aromatic cooking vegetables – ususally carrots, onions and celery, sometimes turnips or peppers – are coloured in the fat that remains in the pot. The liquid – water, well-flavoured stock or wine or a mix of all three – is then poured in and stirred to incorporate all the rich pan juices left in the pot. Lastly the main ingredient of the dish is returned to the enriched liquid; the pot is covered with a close-fitting lid and the pot roast is simmered until the meat (or poultry or vegetables) being pot roasted is done. The last stage is to skim excess fats from the surface of the cooking liquids, and concentrate the flavours of the sauce by rapidly boiling the pan juices to reduce them to half the original quantity.

Portuguese Pot Roast

Portuguese Pot Roast cooks a joint of beef on a bed of sliced carrots, onions and leeks with a generous bouquet garni, a little paprika, 2-4 tablespoons of golden syrup and a cup or two of stock or water.

4 lbs rolled top rump of beef (tied in 1 piece)
4 tablespoons olive oil
2-4 tablespoons golden syrup
salt and freshly ground pepper
crushed dried chillies
300ml/½ pint well-flavoured beef stock
1 tablespoon butter
1 tablespoon pepper

Garnish:
4-6 medium sized potatoes
4 bunches baby carrots, sliced
2-4 stalks celery, cut into sticks
8-12 small onions
4-6 hard boiled eggs, sliced
1 bunch green asparagus, cut into
  4cm/1 ½ inch segments

Marinade:
½ bottle red wine
4 large carrots, cut into 4cm/1 ½- inch
  segments
2 large Spanish onions, cut into quarters
2 leeks, cut into 4cm/1 ½ inch segments
2 strips orange peel
2 tablespoons olive oil
2 cloves garlic, finely chopped
1 teaspoon salt
1 teaspoon paprika
½ teaspoon freshly ground pepper
2 bay leaves
2 cloves

1 Preheat the oven to 150°C/325°F/Gas 2. Place the tied rump of beef in a large porcelaine bowl, or stainless steel casserole just large enough to hold it. Add the marinade ingredients and marinate the beef overnight, turning it at least once.

2 When ready to cook, heat the olive oil and golden syrup in a large heatproof casserole; add the beef and brown it well on all sides. Then add the marinade, complete with vegetables and aromatics. Cover and cook in the oven for 1 hour. Remove the casserole from the oven; turn the meat over, add the beef stock, season with salt, freshly ground pepper and crushed dried chillies, to taste. Return the casserole to the oven and continue cooking until tender (1 G -1 I hours).

3 Prepare the vegetables garnish: saute sliced potatoes in a little olive oil until golden brown. Poach the carrots until crisp tender. Poach the celery sticks. Poach the asparagus segments. Boil the small onions.

4 To serve: Transfer the beef to a heated serving dish and keep warm. Strain pan juices and thicken with flour; correct seasoning. Arrange fried potatoes, cooked carrots, celery sticks and small onions, halved boiled eggs and cooked asparagus tips around meat. Pour a little sauce over roast. Serve remaining sauce separately.

Pot Roast of Beef with Mushrooms

SERVES 6-8

1.8kg/4lb joint of topside of beef
50g/2oz butter
2 tablespoons olive oil
4 large carrots, finely chopped
4 Spanish onions, finely chopped
2 sprigs parsley
2 sprigs thyme or ½ level teaspoon
  dried thyme
2 small bay leaves

8 ripe tomatoes, quartered and seeded
600ml/1 pint well-flavoured beef stock
8-10 tablespoons red wine
Salt and freshly ground pepper
450g/1lb button mushrooms, thinly sliced
185ml/7 fl oz double cream
6-8 tablespoons Madeira
Juice of ½ lemon

1 Preheat oven (110°C/ 225°F/ Gas ¼).

2 Melt butter with olive oil in a heavy, 3 litre/5 or 6 pint casserole, and brown meat richly and evenly over a steady, moderate heat, together with finely chopped carrots and onions.

3 When meat is thoroughly browned all over, add herbs and quartered, seeded tomatoes. Pour in beef stock and wine and season to taste with salt and freshly ground pepper. Bring to simmering point over a low heat. Cover pan tightly and transfer to the oven. Cook for about 2½ hours, with the pan juices barely at simmering point, turning joint and basting it occasionally with its own pan juices.

4 When meat is tender, remove it from the pan and keep hot.

5 Skim pan juices of excess fat if necessary, and rub juices and vegetables through a fine sieve. Pour back into the casserole and boil vigorously, stirring, until reduced by one half.

6 Return meat to the casserole together with sliced mushrooms. Bring to simmering point again. Replace cover and return casserole to the oven (or simmer very, very gently on top of the stove) for about 45 minutes longer to finish cooking and allow flavours to develop .

7 Just before serving, lift out the meat, allowing juices to drain back into casserole. Slice meat thickly and arrange on a heated serving platter. Keep hot.

8 To finish sauce: add double cream and Madeira, and simmer over a low heat until slightly thickened, stirring constantly and scraping bottom and sides of casserole with a wooden spoon. Correct seasoning, adding more salt or freshly ground pepper and a squeeze of lemon juice if necessary. Strain sauce.

9 Spoon some of the sauce over beef slices and serve remainder separately in a heated sauce bowl.

Pot Roasted Duck with Turnips

SERVES 4

1 tender duck
2 tablespoons flour
Salt and freshly ground pepper
4 tablespoons butter
16 baby turnips (or 4-6 young turnips quartered)

1-2 tablespoons castor sugar
800ml/ 1½ pints well-flavoured stock
1 bouquet garni
1 Spanish onion, quartered
Lemon juice

1 Prepare and truss the duck as for roasting. Dust with 1 tablespoon flour and season inside and out with salt and freshly ground pepper. Melt the butter in a heat-proof casserole and sauté the duck on all sides until it is nicely browned.

2 Remove the duck from the casserole and add the baby turnips (or quartered turnips) to the juices in the casserole. Sprinkle with sugar and simmer turnips, stirring until lightly coloured. Remove and keep warm.

3 Add remaining flour to the fat left in the casserole and stir until smooth. Pour in the stock; bring to the boil and skim; add the bouquet garni and quartered onion. Season with lemon juice and salt and pepper to taste.

4 Return the duck to the casserole; cover and cook gently for 30 to 35 minutes. Add the turnips and continue cooking about 30 minutes longer, or until the duck and turnips are tender, turning duck occasionally during cooking time.

5 When ready to serve: Transfer the duck to a hot serving dish; remove strings and arrange turnips around duck. Skim fat from pan juices; reduce sauce over a high heat and strain over and around the duck.

Cooking au Gratin

The term *au gratin* (from the French verb *gratiner*: to brown) applies to oven-cooked dishes (macaroni, noodles, *gnocchi*, meats, fish and vegetables) baked in shallow, heatproof *gratin* dishes, usually covered with a sauce, sprinkled liberally with breadcrumbs, dotted with butter and browned in the oven or under the grill. (When browning in the oven, it is wise to set the dish in a pan half full of simmering water, to prevent the sauce from spoiling or separating.)

Although dishes *au gratin* are generally associated with cheese, this is not an essential ingredient.

Left-overs (poached fish, chicken or turkey and sliced hard-boiled eggs) make an excellent luncheon or supper dish when cooked *au gratin*.

Fish and shellfish

Gratins can be made with either raw fish or leftovers. The most common raw, fish-based *gratins* are made with whole fish, fish fillets or fish steaks, first sautéed in butter or poached in a little concentrated fish stock for a few minutes. They are then covered with a sauce *duxelles* (finely chopped mushrooms, onion and parsley, sautéed until smooth in butter) or a well-flavoured cream or cheese sauce, and sprinkled with freshly grated breadcrumbs and Parmesan cheese. Or, a little sauce Béchamel (see page 29) may be poured around the fish before it is dotted with butter and sprinkled with chopped parsley, mushrooms, shallots and cheese.

Vegetables

Most vegetables can be *gratinéed*. *Gratin dauphinois* (thinly sliced new potatoes, cream and grated cheese, browned in the oven until smooth and flavourful, with a crisp golden crust) is a wonderful accompaniment to steaks and roasts. *Gratin savoyard* exchanges beef stock for cream in an equally delicious variation of this great dish. Or try adding diced celery, finely chopped onions or shallots, or a hint of garlic to this basic recipe. You will be delighted with the result.

Larousse Gastronomique (published in the United Kingdom by Paul Hamlyn) talks of a delicious *gratin languedocien* of peeled and sliced aubergines and tomato halves sautéed in olive oil, then placed in alternate layers in a buttered baking dish. The vegetables are covered with a mixture of fresh breadcrumbs and finely chopped garlic and parsley, sprinkled with olive oil (or dotted with butter), brought to the boil on the top of the stove and then baked slowly in the oven till the top is crisp and well browned.

Other vegetables (French beans, broccoli, endive, celery, leeks, onion and marrows) can be *gratinéed* in a similar fashion.

Creamed Eggs au Gratin

SERVES 2

4 hard-boiled eggs, sliced
2 tablespoons butter
2 tablespoons flour
150ml/¼ pint milk
150ml/¼ pint double cream
Salt and freshly ground pepper

1 egg yolk, beaten
2 tablespoons whipped cream
Fresh breadcrumbs
Freshly grated cheese
Butter

1 Melt 2 tablespoons butter in a saucepan. Add flour and cook until the roux just starts to turn golden. Add milk and cook, stirring constantly, until sauce is reduced to half the original quantity. Stir in double cream.

2 Add 300ml/½ pint of this sauce to sliced hard-boiled eggs. Season to taste with a little salt and freshly ground pepper and pour into a heatproof *gratin* dish.

3 Combine the remaining sauce with the beaten egg yolk, fold in whipped cream and spread over creamed egg mixture. Sprinkle with fresh breadcrumbs and freshly grated cheese. Dot with butter and brown in a hot oven (230°C/450°F/Gas 8) or under the grill. Serve immediately.

Crab Ramekins

SERVES 4

300g/12 oz fresh crab meat
4 slices white bread, crusts removed
225ml/8 fl oz double cream
½ teaspoon dry mustard
Salt and freshly ground pepper
1 teaspoon Worcestershire sauce

Tabasco sauce
Softened butter or oil
2 tablespoons fresh white breadcrumbs
2 tablespoons freshly grated parmesan
2 tablespoons melted butter

1 Preheat the oven to 190°C/375°F/Gas 5.

2 Remove all the tendons and bits of shell from the crab meat and place in a bowl.

3 Dice the bread.

4 In a bowl combine the double cream and dry mustard and season with salt and freshly ground pepper to taste. Stir in the Worcestershire sauce and then stir in the diced bread. Gently fold in the crab meat, add Tabasco sauce to taste, correct the seasoning if necessary.

5 Brush ramekins with softened butter or oil. Spoon the crabmeat mixture into 4 individual 150ml/ ¼ pint ramekins or soufflé dishes and sprinkle evenly with fresh white breadcrumbs and grated parmesan and the melted butter. Place in the preheated oven and bake for 10-15 minutes or until golden. Serve immediately.

Gratin of Scallops and Leeks

SERVES 4-6

16 scallops
550g/1 ¼ lb leeks
Salt
Butter
8 tablespoons double cream

Freshly ground pepper
Cayenne pepper
Grated nutmeg
2-4 tablespoons melted butter

1 Remove scallops from their shells. Discard the black piece sticking to it and the little tube trailing from the end. Wash in cold running water to rid them of sand. Drain and dry carefully.

2 Separate the white section of each scallop from the orange coral and cut in half.

3 Clean leeks and plunge into boiling salted water. When water returns to the boil, cook for 3-5 minutes, according to size of leeks (they should still be firm). Drain. Press dry with a clean kitchen towel to remove excess moisture.

4 Cut leeks into 2.5cm/1inch pieces and arrange in the bottom of a well-buttered gratin dish.

5 Arrange coral and sliced scallops on top of leeks. Moisten with double cream and season generously with salt, freshly ground pepper, cayenne pepper and grated nutmeg to taste. Spoon over melted butter and cook in a hot oven (230°C/450°F/Gas 8) for 7-10 minutes. Serve immediately.

Cooking 'En Papillote'

Cooking 'en papillote' is really only half-cooking. When you enclose an ingredient in a papillote, it is already half-cooked, or has at the very least been 'seized' in hot fat before being folded into the paper case (or foil packet) which gives this process its name.

A *papillote* is just a folded piece of thin parchment paper or aluminium foil, about 22 x 27.5 cm/8½ by 11 inches, cut into an oval or heart shape, greased with oil or butter and then crimped to enclose the ingredient to be cooked.

Cooking 'en papillote' is not only colourful but gastronomic, for the ingredient cooked in this way simmers gently in its own juices, hermetically sealed, so it loses none of its special flavour and aroma. It is almost always necessary to flavour and colour the ingredient to be cooked in parchment paper (or foil) in a little butter or oil before enclosing it in its casing, but it is important not to cook it too much in this preliminary process or you lose the advantages and virtues of this exciting cooking method.

Nothing adds more glamour to a meal than individual servings of trout, red mullet or sole, veal cutlets, veal chops, or fat slices of salmon or turbot, first coloured in a little butter or oil, seasoned with freshly ground pepper, salt, fresh herbs and finely chopped shallots and mushrooms. The whole is then enclosed in its prepared paper case, which is fried for a moment in hot oil to colour and puff the case, and then cooked in the oven. Serve your papillotes in their puffed paper shells and let guests cut them open at the table with a knife. Aluminium foil cases are cooked in the oven only and the foil is removed before the finished dishes are served at the table.

To cook 'en papillote'

1 Fold parchment paper in half and cut paper into an oval, or heart shape, large enough to enclose, when folded, the food to be cooked.

2 Brush the insides of the paper shapes with melted butter or oil.

3 Sauté the food for a few moments to colour it before placing in paper or aluminium shapes.

4 Place food on one half of paper shape. Add butter and aromatics (finely chopped onion, shallot and mushrooms) and season to taste with salt and freshly ground pepper.

If papillote is paper: Fold shapes and seal edges well by crimping them together. A little beaten egg white can help here. Paper shells can be puffed up by frying for a minute or two in hot oil in a frying pan. Then put shells on a baking sheet in the oven where they will keep the puffed-up appearance while the ingredients continue to cook.

If papillote is foil: Fold shapes and seal edges well by crimping them together. Put shells on a baking sheet in the oven where they will continue to cook.

Saumon en Papillote

SERVES 2

2 thick salmon steaks
Salt and freshly ground pepper
6 tablespoons butter
16 thin strips of carrot,
 7cm/3 inches long
16 thin strips of cucumber,
 7cm/3 inches long
Groundnut oil

16 strips of spring onion (green parts
 only), 7cm/3 inches long
4-6 fresh tarragon leaves
4 tablespoons dry white wine
2 tablespoons reduced chicken stock
Sauce Hollandaise (see page 33) or
 fresh lemon wedges
Beaten egg white

1 Season the salmon steaks with salt and freshly ground pepper and sauté steaks in the butter until seared on both sides. Transfer seared steaks to a serving dish and cool.

2 Add strips of carrot and cucumber to pan and sauté vegetables for 5-8 minutes, or until vegetables are just crisp, stirring constantly to prevent them from browning or sticking to the pan. Season with salt and freshly ground pepper to taste. Remove from heat. Cool.

3 Cut 4 large oval sheets of greaseproof paper, approximately 17 x 27.5 cm/7 x 11 inches. Brush paper ovals on one side with groundnut oil. Place 2 paper ovals, oiled side up, on working surface; place half the carrot and cucumber strips in the centre of each oval. Then place a salmon steak on top of vegetables. Arrange half the spring onion strips in cavity of each steak and top each steak with 2 thin slices of butter and 2-3 fresh tarragon leaves. Add 2 tablespoons white wine and 1 tablespoon reduced chicken stock for added flavour to each steak.

4 Preheat oven to 190°C/375°F/Gas 5. Close the *papillotes* by placing the remaining paper ovals, oiled side down, over the salmon and vegetables, and crimping the edges of the paper ovals together carefully, making sure that each *papillote* is well sealed. (Brush a little beaten egg white on the edges before crimping to facilitate this.)

5 Oil a baking tray with groundnut oil and put it into the preheated oven for 5 minutes; place the p*apillotes* on the heated tray, brush with groundnut oil and cook for 20 minutes.

6 To serve salmon steaks: bring *papillotes* to the table and open each *papillote* with a pair of sharp scissors or a very sharp knife. Place each *papillote* on a heated dish. Accompany with sauce Hollandaise or fresh lemon wedges.

Red Mullet en Papillote

SERVES 4 AS AN APPETISER

4 small red mullet, 100-125g/
   4-5 oz each
Olive oil
Salt and freshly ground pepper
4 bay leaves
4 thin slices bacon, grilled
Fat or oil, for frying
4 slices lemon
4 anchovy fillets

Sauce
4-5 egg whites
300 ml/½ pint double cream
4-5 anchovy fillets, mashed
Salt and freshly ground pepper
Freshly grated nutmeg

1 Sprinkle cleaned and scaled fish with olive oil and season to taste with salt and freshly ground pepper. Place bay leaf on one side of fish and a thin slice of grilled bacon on the other side.

2 Cut 4 pieces of greaseproof paper, approximately 22 x 27.5cm/8½ x 11 inches; fold each piece in half and cut into 'heart' shape. Open out and brush with olive oil. Place prepared fish, bay leaf and bacon on one half. Fold paper shape over and seal edges well by crimping them together.

3 Sauté *papillotes* in deep fat or oil for about 18 minutes.

4 To make sauce: Beat egg whites until stiff, and whip cream. Combine the two and add mashed anchovy fillets, and salt, freshly ground pepper, and nutmeg to taste. Cook over simmering water, stirring constantly, until sauce is just heated through. Strain and keep warm.

5 When *papillotes* are cooked, arrange them on a serving dish. Open each carefully and decorate fish with a slice of lemon and an anchovy fillet. Serve with sauce.

Vitello al Cartoccio

(Italian Veal Chops in a Paper Case)

SERVES 4

4 veal chops, 2.5cm/1 inch thick
8-12 button mushrooms, thinly
sliced
2 tablespoons butter
4 tablespoons olive oil
4-6 ripe tomatoes, peeled, seeded
and diced
2 slices cooked ham, cut in
matchstick-length strips

¾ teaspoon dried oregano
Salt and freshly ground pepper
4 tablespoons dry white wine
2 tablespoons finely chopped
parsley
2 tablespoons finely chopped
anchovies
Grated rind of ¾ lemon

1 Sauté sliced mushrooms in 2 tablespoons each butter and olive oil in a large heavy-bottomed frying pan for 3 minutes, stirring constantly. Add tomatoes, ham, oregano, salt and freshly ground pepper to taste, and cook for a minute or two more.

2 Add white wine and bring to the boil. Lower heat and simmer for 10 minutes.

3 Season veal chops with salt and freshly ground pepper. Heat 2 tablespoons olive oil in a large clean frying pan and sauté chops until they are brown on both sides.

4 Cut 4 folded pieces of parchment paper into ovalslarge enough to contain veal chops when folded over. Brush paper on both sides with olive oil. Place 1 veal chop in the centre of each oval section of oiled paper and cover with the sauce. Sprinkle with parsley, anchovy and lemon rind and fold over oval paper, sealing edges well.

5 Place veal packets on a baking sheet. Bake in a preheated oven (190°C/375°F/Gas 5) for 20 minutes, or until chops are tender.

Red Snapper en Papillote

SERVES 1

1 x 225g/8 oz fillets of red snapper
1 blanched carrot, cut into long
* sticks*
½ fennel, sliced
1 blanched courgette, cut into long
* sticks*
1 mushroom, sliced

1 blanched potato, cut into wedges
½ tomato
2 sprigs of thyme
Balsamic vinegar
Olive oil
Salt and freshly ground pepper

1 Preheat oven to 190°C/375°F/Gas 5.

2 Hammer the fillet of red snapper to tenderize it.

3 Prepare a parchment paper *papillote* as above; brush it with oil and lay the fish in the centre of one side of folded parchment. Place the sticks of courgettes, potato wedges, fennel slices, carrots, mushroom and tomato around the red snapper fillet, as in the picture.

4 Season with salt, freshly ground pepper, a little olive oil and a slice of chive flavoured butter (see below).Fold over the other side of the parchment paper oval and crimp edges firmly together (as above).

5 Place papillote on a baking sheet (as above) and Cook for 8-10 minutes and serve immediately.

Chive Butter

4oz butter, slightly softened
4 tablespoons chives, finely chopped

Juice of ½ lemon
Salt and freshly ground pepper

1 In a mortar, pound the slightly softened butter with the finely chopped chives until well mixed. Add the lemon juice and salt and freshly ground pepper, to taste. Form butter into a loose sausage, wrap in clingfilm and roll into smooth sausage shape. Chill until ready to serve.

2 To serve chive butter: Remove clingfilm; trim ends and cut butter into 0.5cm/¼ inch rounds.

Beef Strips en Papillote

SERVES 4

*450g/1 lb rump or sirloin steak,
2.5cm/1 inch thick
Oil or melted butter, for brushing
Salt and freshly ground pepper
50g/2 oz butter
2 red peppers, thinly sliced
½ Spanish onion, finely chopped
225g/8 oz button mushrooms,
    thinly sliced*

Roquefort butter:
*50g/2 oz butter
1 tablespoon flour
25g/1 oz Roquefort cheese, crumbled
2 tablespoons finely chopped parsley
Lemon juice*

Garnish
Sprigs of watercress

1 Heat the oven to 190°C/375°F/Gas 5. To make Roquefort butter: In a small bowl, mash the butter and flour with a wooden spoon. Add the crumbled Roquefort cheese and parsley and mash again. Add lemon juice, to taste, then place mixture on a piece of greaseproof paper. Pat mixture into an oblong, wrap with the paper and chill in the refrigerator until ready to use.

2 Brush the steak on both sides with oil or melted butter and sprinkle with freshly ground pepper. Heat a frying pan and fry the steak for 2-3 minutes, turning once, until browned on both sides. Remove the steak from the pan and cut it, across the grain, in 16-20 thin strips. Season the steak strips with salt and freshly ground pepper to taste. Add the red peppers to the pan and sauté briefly. Remove.

3 Melt 25g/1 oz of the butter in a frying pan and sauté the finely chopped onion until transparent. Add the rest of the butter, and when melted, add the sliced mushrooms. Sauté for 2-3 minutes, then season to taste with salt and freshly ground pepper.

4 Cut 4 x 28cm/11inch squares of double thickness foil. Place one-eighth of the onion and mushroom mixture in the centre of each square of foil. Arrange 4 or 5 steak strips on each square of foil, along with the red peppers, and cover with the remaining onion and mushroom mixture. Top each with a quarter of the chilled Roquefort butter.

5 Seal the foil packets neatly and securely so that no juices can escape during cooking. Arrange the parcels on a baking tray, join upwards, and cook in the oven for 15 minutes. When cooked, undo the foil wrappings and garnish the steak with sprigs of watercress to serve.

Composite Cooking

Composite cooking might be a new cooking term in your culinary lexicon. It simply means making light work out of complicated dishes by combining top-of-the-stove cooking - whether in a non-stick frying pan or a ridged grill pan - with oven cooking, to ensure maximum flavour and tenderness in the foods being cooked without the worry of over-searing or over-charring.

Composite cooking is a professional term for a simple cooking process used by professional cooks to ensure that tastes remain pure and cooking remains simple. So simple in fact, that you will wonder why you never used this cooking method before.

Composite cooking requires no special equipment other than (1) a non-stick frying pan, or sauté pan, or a ridged grill pan for pan-frying, sautéeing or pan-grilling meats, fish and poultry before finishing it off in the oven, and (2) a pre-heated oven, set at 240°C/475°F/Gas 9, before you start cooking.

Composite cooking is, in fact, a two-level cooking technique that lets you pan-fry, sauté or pan grill on top of the stove while a sauce is simmering in another saucepan ready to be added to the dish at the last minute, a trick of the trade that cuts away the inessentials of a dish to get to the flavourful essence. Once you experiment with this easy way of cooking, you will never look back. Veal and pork, for example, are two white meats that benefit enormously from composite cooking: both meats require colouring and the sealing in of the juices of the meat in butter or olive oil, or a combination of the two, before being transferred to a preheated oven to continue cooking without the danger of over-browning or over-charring as they cook to moist tenderness in the oven. Another plus here is the fact that you can now add a squeeze of lemon juice or a tablespoon of *glace de viande* (greatly reduced meat essence or gravy, see page 23) or a sepatately cooked savoury sauce to bring added excitement to your cooking.

For pan-fried or pan-grilled fish steaks or fillets, cook them for a minute or two on each side (just enough to colour them and give them flavour) and then finish them in the oven for a further few minutes to give them maximum moisture and flavour. This is quick cooking at its very best.

Stuffed Trout with Meursault

Guinea Fowl with Exotic Fruits

Trout Stuffed with Meursault

SERVES 6

7 fresh trout (225g/½lb each)
6 large mushrooms, finely chopped
1 finely-chopped black truffle
(optional)
2 tablespoons butter
1 egg white
Salt and freshly ground pepper
150-300ml/¼–½ pint
double cream
300ml/½ pint fish stock
300ml/½ pint Meursault, or other
dry white wine

6 shallots, finely chopped
Truffle slices (optional)

Sauce
150ml/¼ pint fish veloute (fish stock
thickened with 1 tablespoon each butter
and flour)
300ml/½ pint double cream
1 egg yolk
Few drops lemon juice
1 tablespoon butter
Beurre manie (*see below)

1 Slit 6 trout carefully down the back and bone and empty them. Fillet 7th trout. Sauté finely-chopped mushrooms and truffle in 2 tablespoons butter.

2 Pound meat of filleted trout to a smooth paste in a mortar, then pass through a fine sieve and pound in mortar again with raw egg white. Season to taste with salt and freshly ground pepper.

3 Place mixture in a bowl, over ice, for 1 hour, gradually working in cream by mixing with a spatula from time to time. Add sautéed mushrooms and truffles to this mixture and stuff fish. Reserve.

4 Just before serving, submerge stuffed trout in fish stock and Meursault in a heatproof shallow casserole; add shallots and salt and pepper to taste. Bring to the boil; cover casserole, remove from heat and allow trout to cook in the heat of the pan itself for 10 minutes. When trout are cooked, place on a heated serving dish; garnish with a few truffle slices and pour over sauce.

To make sauce:
Reduce cooking liquid over a high flame to ¼ original quantity; add fish velouté mixed with double cream and egg yolk. Whisk in a few drops of lemon juice and butter. *If sauce seems too thin, thicken with a little *beurre manie* made by mixing equal quantities of flour and butter to a smooth paste. Heat until sauce is smooth and thick, stirring constantly. Strain over fish and serve immediately.

Guinea Fowl with Exotic Fruits

SERVES 4

4 Guinea fowl breasts
2 tablespoons olive oil
2 tablespoons butter
Sea salt and freshly ground pepper
Crushed dried chillies
4 passion fruits, cut in half
4 tablespoons dry white wine

4 tablespoons Madeira
4 tablespoons diced butter
100g/4 oz pineapple cubes
1 papaya, peeled and diced
1 kiwi fruit, peeled and diced
100g/4 oz strawberries, halved

1 Preheat oven to 180°C/350°F/Gas 4.

2 In an ovenproof casserole heat the olive oil and the butter.

3 Season the guinea fowl breasts with sea salt, freshly ground pepper and crushed dried chillies.

4 Brown the guinea fowl on all sides in the hot fat, then place casserole in the preheated oven for 35 minutes or until the juices run clear when pierced with a skewer.

To prepare the sauce
5 Remove the flesh from the passion fruit and sieve into a small bowl.

6 In a small saucepan, combine the sieved passion fruit juice with the wine and Madeira. Reduce to approximately half the original quantity and gradually whisk in the butter.

7 Remove the guinea fowl from the oven. Place on a warmed serving dish.

8 Strain the guinea fowl pan juices into the sauce. Heat gently over a medium heat, add diced fruits and heat gently to warm the fruits.

9 Garnish the guinea fowl breasts with warm exotic fruits and sauce and serve immediately.

Note: Fruits may be sliced instead of diced, if preferred.

Beefsteak Pizzaiola

SERVES 4

4 steaks
Olive oil
Salt and freshly ground pepper

Pizzaiola sauce
4 garlic cloves, finely chopped

6 tablespoons olive oil
1 large Spanish onion, thinly sliced
1 large can Italian peeled tomatoes
Salt and freshly ground pepper
Crushed dried chillies
Dried oregano

1 Brush the steaks with olive oil; season with freshly ground pepper and grill the steaks from 4-6 minutes on each side, or more, according to the rareness you prefer.

2 When the steaks are sealed, season with salt and a little more freshly ground pepper. Remove from heat and reserve.

3 Transfer the steaks to the sauce in the frying pan and let them cook for 3-4 minutes longer in the sauce. Turn the steaks once. Serve immediately.

To make Pizzaiola sauce:
In a large frying pan, sauté chopped garlic in olive oil for 1 minute; add the sliced Spanish onion and continue to cook, stirring, until the vegetables are translucent. Then add Italian peeled tomatoes and cook over a medium heat, stirring from time to time, until the sauce is reduced to one third the original quantity. Season with salt, freshly ground pepper, crushed dried chillies and dried oregano, to taste.

Success with Vegetables

Vegetables are important to our diet for their nutrition and vitamin content. Well-prepared vegetables not only taste better, but retain more of these important nutrients and vitamins than those soaked in water. The key to successful vegetable cookery is a minimum of water and cooking time in order to retain maximum flavour and texture. To me, the overcooking of vegetables is the eighth deadly sin . . . and should be punished accordingly.

So, do not drown vegetables in water. Instead, cook them in a little butter or olive oil, with just enough water, chicken stock, white wine or even steam to bring out their delicate flavours and textures. And serve them slightly crisp, not reduced to a pulpy, colourless mass.

Take care over the selection and storage of your vegetables. Cooks with their own kitchen gardens are to be envied - new potatoes brought in fresh from the garden, peas picked an hour before serving, tomatoes still warm from the vine, all add so much to the savour of good eating. But if you can't grow your own vegetables, shop carefully for them, and select those that are crisp, fresh-looking and colourful. Limp, tired vegetables will have lost their texture, much of their flavour and most of their goodness, and no amount of cooking and attention will revive them.

Don't peel vegetables unless it is absolutely necessary. It is true that most of the goodness is right under the skin, or in the skin itself. I usually wash vegetables with a stiff vegetable brush, or, in the case of mushrooms, tomatoes and very new potatoes, just wipe them with a damp cloth. They are then stored in plastic bags or boxes in the refrigerator to keep them crisp and fresh until ready to be used. Parsley and other herbs will keep green and fresh in this way for weeks.

Keep a vegetable juice jar (covered) in the refrigerator. Any liquid left over from cooking vegetables can be strained into the jar, to be used later as wonderful flavour additives for soups, sauces and stews.

Italian Cauliflower Sauté

SERVES 4

1 medium-sized cauliflower	Freshly ground pepper
Salt	2 tablespoons finely chopped
Lemon juice	parsley
4 tablespoons olive oil	Lemon quarters

1 To prepare cauliflower: Cut off stem and remove green leaves from a medium-sized cauliflower. Soak the head for 30 minutes in cold water to which you have added ½ level teaspoon salt and the juice of ½ lemon. Drain, and break (or cut) cauliflower into florets.

2 To cook cauliflower: Fill a deep saucepan with enough water to cover florets. Add ½ teaspoon salt and bring to the boil. Put florets in boiling water and simmer gently for 8-10 minutes. Drain.

3 Heat olive oil in a frying pan, add drained florets and sauté until lightly coloured. Season with freshly ground pepper and lemon juice, to taste.

4 Serve sautéed cauliflower immediately, garnished with finely chopped parsley and lemon quarters.

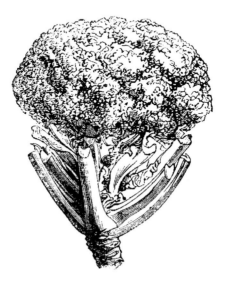

Buttered Glazed Vegetables

SERVES 4

*450g/1lb small white onions, small
   carrots or small turnips
4 tablespoons butter*

*4 tablespoons chicken stock
1 tablespoon sugar
Salt*

1 Peel onions, carrots or turnips and place them in a small saucepan.

2 Cover with cold water and cook over high heat until water boils. Remove from heat and drain.

3 Replace onions, carrots or turnips in saucepan. Add butter and chicken stock, season with sugar and salt to taste, and simmer over low heat until vegetables have absorbed the liquid without burning and taken on a little colour.

4 Remove the vegetables from the pan and serve immediately.

Note: A combination of buttered glazed vegetables, each cooked individually as in the picture, makes a delicious vegetable course on its own.

Country-fried Potatoes

900g/2lb large new potatoes
1 medium-sized onion, finely
chopped
4 slices bacon, finely chopped

1 tablespoon butter
3 tablespoons olive oil
Salt and freshly ground pepper
2 tablespoons finely chopped parsley

1 Scrub potatoes clean. Peel them and cut them into 0.5cm/¼-inch dice.

2 Sauté onion and bacon in butter and 1 tablespoon olive oil until onion is golden, 4-5 minutes. Put aside.

3 In a large, heavy frying pan, heat remaining olive oil and sauté diced potatoes over a high heat until crisp and golden on all sides. Season to taste with salt and freshly ground pepper.

4 Return sautéed onion and bacon to the pan, toss lightly to mix thoroughly with the potatoes and sauté for 1 minute longer. Serve immediately with finely chopped parsley.

Pommes Anna

SERVES 4

450g /1 lb new potatoes
4-6 tablespoons softened butter

Salt and freshly ground pepper

1 Peel and slice potatoes thinly and soak in cold water for a few minutes. Drain and dry thoroughly.

2 Butter a shallow heatproof copper or enamelled iron casserole with lid (French chefs use a special thick copper '*pommes anna*' pan) and in it place a layer of sliced potatoes overlapping on bottom and around sides of casserole. Spread potatoes with 1 tablespoon softened butter and season to taste with salt and freshly ground pepper. Repeat layers as above, with a final spreading of butter on top.

3 Cover casserole and cook in a fairly hot oven (220°C/425°F/Gas 7) for 45 minutes to 1 hour, or until potatoes are brown around outside edges.

4 To serve, invert golden brown potato 'cake' on to a heated serving dish.

Three Hot Vegetable Purées

SERVES 4–6

700g/1½lb frozen peas or
450g/1lb frozen sweetcorn or
700g/1½lb fresh carrots,
  thinly sliced
4 tablespoons chicken stock
4 tablespoons butter

1-2 tablespoons instant potato
  powder
1-2 tablespoons double cream
Salt and freshly ground pepper
Lemon juice and sugar (optional)

1 Place frozen peas or sweetcorn or thinly sliced raw carrots in a pan. Add chicken stock and butter.

2 Bring to the boil. Push a sheet of greaseproof paper down into pan on top of vegetables, reduce heat to moderate and simmer until very tender – about 5 minutes for frozen vegetables, 10–12 minutes for carrots.

3 Pour contents of pan into a blender. Add instant potato powder. Turn to maximum speed and blend for 2 minutes, stopping occasionally to scrape down sides of goblet with a spatula. (Or put vegetables through a mouli or rub through a sieve. In the case of sweetcorn, return contents of sieve to purée to give it bulk and texture.)

4 Return purée to pan. Beat vigorously with a wooden spoon over a moderate heat until purée is thoroughly hot again, adding enough cream so it just holds its shape. Season to taste with salt and freshly ground pepper. (Pea purée will be improved by a squeeze of lemon juice, sweetcorn purée by ½ level teaspoon sugar.) Serve immediately.

Note: if you wish, reserve a tablespoon or two of the cooked peas or sweetcorn kernels for garnish. Carrot purée looks well with a garnish of finely chopped parsley.

Corn and Red Pepper Pancakes

SERVES 6

3 tablespoons butter
3 tablespoons flour
400g/14oz can creamed sweetcorn
1 egg yolk
4-6 tablespoons crème fraîche
Salt and freshly ground pepper

Crushed dried chillies
1 red pepper, cored, seeded and diced
185g/7oz can sweetcorn kernels, drained
1 egg white, stiffly beaten
Butter
Crème fraîche

1 In a medium-sized saucepan, melt the butter and add 3 tablespoons flour. Cook for 1–2 minutes, stirring to form a pale roux. Add the creamed sweetcorn; bring to the boil and reduce the heat to a simmer. Cook for 5 minutes.

2 Remove from the heat; stir in the egg yolk and crème fraîche and season highly with salt, freshly ground pepper and crushed dried chillies to taste. Add the diced red pepper and the drained sweetcorn kernels. Chill until ready to cook.

3 When ready to cook: Remove pancake mixture form the refrigerator. Fold in beaten egg white. Cook on a buttered griddle (use a Swedish iron *plattar* pan with indentations for little pancakes). The pancakes should not be more than 7cm/3 inches in diameter. Serve with crème fraîche.

Brussels Sprouts with Buttered Breadcrumbs

SERVES 4

450g/1lb small brussels sprouts
Salt and freshly ground pepper
4–6 tablespoons toasted breadcrumbs
½ clove garlic, finely chopped
4 tablespoons butter
Lemon juice

Garnish:
2 tablespoons finely chopped
  flat-leafed parsley
Whites of 2 hard-boiled eggs
Thin lemon slices

1 Add sprouts to boiling salted water and simmer uncovered for 5 minutes. Cover pan and continue to cook for 7 (if very young) to 15 minutes longer, or until just tender.

2 Drain well and season generously with salt and freshly ground pepper.

3 Combine hot seasoned sprouts in a frying pan with toasted breadcrumbs and finely chopped garlic and sauté in butter until breadcrumbs are golden. Transfer to a heated serving dish; sprinkle with lemon juice, finely chopped flat-leafed parsley and hard-boiled egg whites; season to taste. Garnish with thin lemon slices.

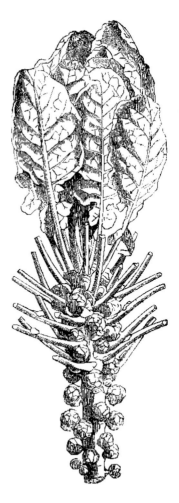

Courgette Soufflés

SERVES 4 AS VEGETABLE

4 medium-sized courgettes
Butter
Salt and freshly ground pepper
150ml/¼ pint bechamel sauce (see page 29)

1 egg yolk
Freshly grated Parmesan cheese
2 egg whites

1 Wash courgettes and cut them in half lengthwise. Scoop out flesh with a spoon, taking care not to pierce shells.

2 Cook courgette pulp in 1 tablespoon butter until reduced to a thick purée. Season generously with salt and freshly ground pepper.

3 Butter a baking dish that will hold courgette shells comfortably side by side.

4 Make a bechamel sauce. Remove sauce from heat and beat in egg yolk. Add cooked courgette pulp and freshly grated Parmesan cheese, to taste. Check seasoning.

5 Preheat oven to 325°F/ 160°C/ Gas 3.

6 Whisk egg white until stiff but not dry and fold gently into lukewarm mixture.

7 Arrange courgette shells in the buttered baking dish. Fill, with soufflé mixture and bake for 40 minutes. Serve immediately.

Mexican Vegetable Chili

SERVES 4-6

1 vegetable marrow
4 large courgettes
4 medium carrots
12–18 baby new potatoes
12–18 baby onions
1 yellow pepper
2 tablespoons olive oil
2 tablespoons butter
1 Spanish onion, finely chopped
4 cloves garlic, finely chopped
600 ml/1 pint good beef stock
1 can chopped tomatoes

3–4 tablespoons mild chilli powder
1 tablespoon flour
2 bay leaves
½ teaspoon powdered cumin
½ teaspoon dried oregano
Salt and freshly ground pepper
225gms/8oz peas or 1 can corn
kernels

Garnish:
Boiled red beans
Saffron rice

To prepare vegetables
1 Cut vegetable marrow, courgettes, and carrots into bite-sized pieces. Wash potatoes. Peel baby onions. Remove seeds and pith from pepper; cut into strips.

2 To cook casserole: In a thick bottomed, heat-proof casserole, melt butter in olive oil, add finely chopped onion and garlic and cook over a medium heat until onion and garlic are transparent. Remove from casserole with a slotted spoon. Reserve.

3 Add prepared vegetables to the casserole and toss over a high heat until vegetables begin to change colour.

4 Return onion and garlic to pan, add boiling beef stock and chopped tomatoes and bring back to the boil; skim, then reduce heat to a simmer; cover casserole and simmer for 20 minutes.

5 Blend mild chilli powder with flour in a little of the hot pan juices and stir into the casserole. Add bay leaves, powdered cumin and dried oregano and salt and freshly ground pepper, to taste. Mix well; add peas (or corn) and simmer over a low heat for 10 more minutes, or until vegetables are tender. Check seasoning and serve vegetable chili with boiled red beans and saffron rice.

Note: Use mild chilli powder or Mexican chilli powder for this recipe (available in the spice section of most supermarkets). Do not use chilli powder; it is far too hot.

Simple Rice Pilaff

Cooking Pasta and Rice

According to an old Roman friend of mine pasta, polenta, rice and beans are all God's gifts, created to give pleasure and sustenance to the Italian poor. When I lived in Italy just after the war, in the teeming, narrow streets of old Rome around the Pantheon, we used to rely on these basic foods as the delicious mainstays of living. Wonderful dishes of spaghetti and *tagliatelle* served with a hundred delicate sauces were the order of the day; or *ravioli* or *tortellini*, tossed with thick, hot cream and freshly grated Parmesan cheese.

Then there were risottos, great dishes of Italian rice simmered gently with chicken stock subtly flavoured with saffron, onion and beef marrow and spiked with wild mushrooms or diced sweetbreads. *Risotto al frutti di mare*, saffron rice tossed with tiny nuggets of fresh seafood - lobster, prawns, shrimp or tiny squid - was a favourite, too.

Finally, there were the great rustic casseroles based on red kidney beans, white *haricot* beans, large flat beans from Sienna or the delicate pink *borlotti*, beans, soaked overnight, then simmered with olive oil and wine, finely chopped garlic and onion, fresh herbs and dried orange peel, and enriched with every kind of pork product imaginable. I liked, too, the Italian way with dried lentils, cooked in the same way, with olive oil and aromatics, and studded with fat slices of *cotechino* or *zampone* sausage, or a fine fat partridge.

It is my firm belief that no household should be without its Italian-inspired emergency store, well stocked with these age-old 'convenience' foods that were well known even in the time of the Caesars.

Rice

In Northern Italy, rice and polenta are usually served in preference to pasta. Italians toss the rice with butter and finely chopped onion, until it begins to be translucent. Then they add rich chicken stock and simmer it gently until it is wonderfully tender - neither mushily soft nor unpleasantly hard, but *al dente*, just like their spaghetti. Then they flavour it with the heady taste of saffron, the earthiness of wild mushrooms, or the crisp texture of golden fried pine nuts.

For best results, rice should be cooked in only as much liquid as it can absorb, and special care taken when serving. The grains mash very easily so, once cooked, they should be tossed lightly with a fork, not stirred with a spoon. Always serve rice as soon as it is cooked.

Simple Rice Pilaff

SERVES 4-6

350 g/12 oz long-grain rice
½ Spanish onion, finely chopped
¼-½ teaspoon turmeric
4 cloves

4 tablespoons butter
450 ml/¾ pint well-flavoured stock
Thyme
Salt and freshly ground pepper

1 Wash rice; drain and dry with a cloth.

2 Sauté finely chopped onion and turmeric in 4 tablespoons butter until light golden. Add rice and cloves and continue to cook, stirring constantly, until rice is translucent. Pour in hot stock, and season to taste with thyme and salt and freshly ground pepper.

3 Cover saucepan and place in the oven (180°C/350°F/Gas 4) for 15-20 minutes, or until the liquid has been absorbed and the rice is tender but not mushy. Serve with additional butter.

Simple Saffron Rice

SERVES 4-6

½ teaspoon powdered saffron
6 tablespoons dry white wine
900ml/1½ pints hot chicken stock
350g/12oz rice

Salt and freshly ground pepper
4 tablespoons butter
Finely chopped parsley

1 Dissolve saffron in white wine. Add it to hot chicken stock and combine in a large saucepan with rice, salt and freshly ground pepper to taste. Cover pan and simmer until all liquid is absorbed and the rice is tender (about 30 minutes).

2 Add butter to hot saffron rice. Garnish with finely chopped parsley and serve immediately.

Butternut Pumpkin or Acorn Squash Risotto

SERVES 4-6

*1 medium sized butternut pumpkin
or acorn squash
300g/10oz risotto rice
1red onion, finely chopped
Butter
1 litre/2 pints hot vegetable stock*

*½–1 teaspoon saffron
Peel of 1 orange, cut into fine julienne strips
Salt and freshly ground pepper
Crushed dried chillies
4 tablespoons toasted pine nuts
4 tablespoons chopped flat leafed parsley*

1 Place two-thirds of the chopped onion in a deep saucepan with 4 tablespoons butter. Cook slowly for 2 to 4 minutes, taking care that the onion does not become brown.

2 Add the rice and cook over a medium heat, stirring constantly with a wooden spoon. After a minute or so, stir in a cup of hot vegetable stock in which you have dissolved the saffron. Add the slivered orange peel and continue cooking, adding stock as needed and stirring from time to time, until rice is cooked thoroughly (15 to 18 minutes). Correct seasoning, adding salt, pepper and crushed dried chillies to taste. By this time all the stock in the pan should have been absorbed by the rice, leaving rice tender but still moist. Stir in cooked cubed butternut pumpkin or acorn squash, toasted pine nuts and the chopped parsley. Heat through and serve immediately.

3 To prepare the butternut pumpkin or acorn squash: cut butternut pumpkin or acorn squash in half. Seed and then cut flesh into cubes. Toss in 2 tablespoons butter with ½ red onion, finely chopped, ¼ vegetable stock cube, crumbled and crushed dried chillies, to taste. Continue to cook until pumpkin or squash cubes are tender.

Pasta

Pasta is really just a dough made to absorb sauce. It is a serious matter in Italy, however, with its own philosophy, traditions, and shapes and sauces for each area. The variety of shapes arises from the fact that each form has its own characteristic way of absorbing the accompanying sauce.

Although there are over 100 different pasta varieties they break down roughly into five groups: (1) ropes or strings – including spaghetti, spaghettini and vermicelli. The sauce for these is usually thick, since the pasta absorbs it on the outside only. (2) Tubes – hollow shapes like macaroni and *rigatoni*. These come in all sizes, and are best with a thinner sauce that flows through the centre hollows. (3) Flats or ribbons – *fettucine*, *tagliatelle* and all kinds of noodles and *lasagne* (4) Envelopes – *ravioli*, *tortellini*, *manicotti* and *cannelloni*, usually stuffed and cooked with a sauce. (5) Pastine – innumerable fancy shapes. The tiny ones are used only in soups.

Properly served in the Italian way, pasta is not fattening. Always serve it in flat soup bowls, designed to keep in the heat, with only 100g/4oz pasta per person, delicately sauced. It should be almost dry, not drowned in a calorie-laden 'soup'. Pasta has the almost magical quality of absorbing and magnifying anything it is served with: Even a simple sauce of olive oil with finely chopped flat-leafed parsley and garlic becomes a thing of beauty when warmed and tossed with a bowl of piping hot spaghetti.

To cook pasta perfectly

Pasta should be cooked in a large quantity of boiling water. Add a tablespoon or two of olive oil to keep the pasta from sticking together or sticking to the bottom of the pan, and 2 good handfuls of salt to flavour it. And no, that is not a lot of salt to use, because we are going to rinse the pasta to rid it of excess starch.

The wonderful Italian expression, *al dente*, means that the pasta is firm and resistant 'to the tooth', cooked through but not mushy. Test if pasta is done by tasting a piece.

Drain pasta in a colander, then run cold water through it to remove excess starch. If you don't do this, the strands are apt to stick together. Have another pot ready with some butter or olive oil in it, in which to toss your drained pasta to warm up again.

Italian Spaghetti with Meatballs

SERVES 4

450g/1 lb spaghetti
Salt
Olive oil
Freshly grated Parmesan cheese
Butter

Meat Balls
350g/12 oz finely chopped veal
225g/8 oz finely chopped prosciutto
  (Parma ham)
2 slices bread, soaked in milk and
  shredded
1 clove garlic, finely chopped
2 tablespoons chopped parsley
Salt and freshly ground pepper
1 egg, lightly beaten

Flour
4 tablespoons olive oil

Sauce
1 Spanish onion, finely chopped
1 clove garlic, finely chopped
2-4 tablespoons olive oil
6-8 button mushrooms, sliced
1 large can peeled tomatoes
6 tablespoons tomato purée
1 bay leaf
1 small strip lemon peel
1 beef stock cube
Salt and freshly ground pepper
1 tablespoon Worcestershire sauce

1 To make meat balls: Combine meat, bread, garlic, parsley, salt, freshly ground pepper and lightly beaten egg. Mix well and shape into small balls. Dredge meat balls with flour and brown on all sides in hot olive oil. Remove from pan and reserve.

2 To make sauce: Sauté onion and garlic in olive oil in a large, thick-bottomed frying pan until transparent. Add sliced mushrooms and sauté for a minute or two more. Add peeled tomatoes, tomato purée, bay leaf, lemon peel and beef stock cube, and season to taste with salt and freshly ground pepper. Simmer gently, covered, for 1 hour, stirring from time to time and adding a little water from time to time, if necessary. Just before serving, stir in Worcestershire sauce.

3 Add meat balls to sauce and simmer gently for 20 minutes.

4 Cook spaghetti in boiling salted water until just tender. Drain.

5 To Serve: Toss spaghetti in a little olive oil over a medium heat to heat through. Arrange meatballs around spagetti; spoon over sauce and sprinkle with freshly grated Parmesan cheese .

Penne with Roasted Pepper and Watercress

SERVES 4

450g/1lb penne (tortiglioni, or
    other tubular pasta)
Salt and freshly ground pepper
2 tablespoons butter
2 tablespoons olive oil
1-2 tablespoons tomato concentrate
1 tub crème fraîche
Freshly grated Parmesan

Garnish:
2 red peppers
1 yellow or orange pepper
Sprigs of fresh watercress

1 To prepare roasted peppers: Roast peppers under the grill, turning them frequently until skins are charred black. Place peppers in a plastic bag and allow to cool enough to handle. Then rub peppers in the bag to loosen charred skins. Remove them from the bag and rub off blackened skins thoroughly under running water, using your fingers, or a small kitchen knife.

2 Cut peppers in half; remove cores and seeds and cut peppers into long strips. Reserve.

3 To prepare watercress: Wash watercress and trim stems. Pat dry. Reserve.

4 To prepare pasta: Bring 1 pot of salted water to the boil. Add penne or pasta of your choice and cook until tender, but still a little firm to the bite. Drain.

5 In a large saucepan, melt butter and olive oil; add penne and toss over a medium heat until pasta is heated through. Add tomato concentrate, salt and freshly ground pepper and toss until pasta is well coloured. Then add crème fraîche and roasted pepper strips and toss over heat until sauce has thickened and warmed through.

6 To serve: Transfer sauced pasta and roasted peppers to a heated serving bowl. Add watercress sprigs, correct seasoning and sprinkle with freshly grated Parmesan cheese. Serve immediately.

Shell Pasta with Parma Ham, Mushrooms and Peas

SERVES 4

*100g/ 4oz stewing veal, finely
  chopped*
50g/ 2oz butter
Salt and freshly ground pepper
5 tablespoons white wine
1 tablespoon tomato concentrate

1 pinch saffron
*100g/ 4oz button mushrooms, finely
  sliced*
2 slices Parma ham, diced
100g/ 4oz frozen peas, defrosted
300g/ 12oz shell pasta or fettucine

1 Prepare the sauce: heat half the butter in a small frying pan and sauté the finely chopped veal over a high heat for 2 minutes or until golden. Season with salt and freshly ground pepper to taste. Pour in the white wine, tomato concentrate and saffron and simmer for 15 minutes.

2 In a medium sized frying pan heat the remaining butter. Add the button mushrooms and the diced Parma ham and saute for 5 minutes or until golden, tossing with a spatula.

3 Strain the wine sauce mixture over the sautéed mushrooms and ham; add the peas and cook for a further 5 minutes. Correct the seasoning, and keep warm.

4 Meanwhile bring a saucepan of salted water to the boil add the shell pasta, or fettucine and boil until *al dente*. Drain and transfer to a serving dish. Pour over the sauce and serve immediately.

Penne with Roasted Pepper and Watercress

Shell Pasta with Parma Ham, Mushrooms and Peas

Salads

I know of no shop in the world other than *Fauchon's* in the *Place de la Madeleine* in Paris which has a greater variety of salads and salad herbs than I used to grow in my Suffolk kitchen garden. I like to use as many fresh greens as I can, to ensure the utmost variety in my salads. Not just ordinary lettuce; young spinach leaves, chicory, endive, corn salad (*mâche*), dark Cos lettuce, Salad Bowl lettuce and Little Gem, with their light green, crinkly leaves, and, of course, rocket, arugula, tarragon, coriander and all the other fresh herbs, all add immeasurably to the pleasure of salad-making.

For the purist, a salad evokes a beautiful vision of wonderful green leaves carefully dried, leaf by leaf, in a clean towel, a salad basket or in one of those machines that dries the leaves by centrifugal force. I don't know why, but I prefer drying my salad greens by hand, perhaps because I always have since I was a very small boy. My job in the family, during the depression years, was to dry the lettuce, leaf by leaf, with a clean kitchen towel. So easy to do.

Oscar Wilde once compared the making of a salad dressing to diplomacy. He said it was really only a question of how much oil you put with your vinegar. I like French olive oil, Italian olive oil or oil from Tunisia or Morocco. If your olive oil does not have that typical fruity olive taste, here is a trick. Just put 2 or 3 black olives (preserved in oil, not brine) in your bottle of olive oil to give a wonderfully fruity flavour to your dressing.

Making a salad dressing is very easy: all we need is a level teaspoon Dijon mustard and 2 tablespoons wine vinegar. We don't put the olive oil in yet because mustard won't dissolve in oil; it has to dissolve first in the wine vinegar to a smooth consistency. Then we flavour the vinegar and mustard mixture with salt and freshly ground pepper. Finally, we add fruity olive oil. The perfect formula is 3 to 1 (3 parts olive oil to 1 part wine vinegar or lemon juice), or, if your vinegar is very strong, 4 parts oil to 1 part vinegar. I like to use red wine vinegar to give a nice healthy outdoors look to the vinaigrette. For a thicker dressing add an ice cube. We can add many many things to this dressing: chopped chives, or a combination of chopped basil, tarragon and chives, for example. Or we could make the dressing for Caesar's salad: just sprinkle a little freshly grated Parmesan cheese over the dressing, with garlic croûtons, finely chopped anchovies and a coddled egg (poached for 1 minute). Finely chopped anchovies, onion and fresh herbs make a very good salad dressing, too. And perhaps one of my favourite tricks is to add a bit of crumbled Roquefort cheese, chopped walnuts and fresh herbs to the dressing for a salad of spinach, watercress, corn salad and lettuce. It's really a peasant salad, which makes a very good first course.

More substantial salads can be served as a first course, or even as a luncheon or supper dish – add sliced tomatoes, diced tuna fish, or sieved hard-boiled eggs to your basic salad. There's a whole world of salads, and each and every one is a delicious adjunct to good dining.

Tossed Green Salad

SERVES 4-6

2 small heads Little Gem lettuce　　*Vinaigrette sauce (see below)*
1 bunch watercress

1 Wash lettuce leaves well in a large quantity of water.

2 Drain leaves well. Dry thoroughly so there is no water on them to dilute the dressing.

3 Wash watercress and cut off stems. Shake dry. Remove any yellowed or damaged leaves.

4 To serve, pour vinaigrette sauce into salad bowl and arrange prepared lettuce leaves and watercress sprigs on top. At the table, toss salad to ensure that every leaf is glistening with dressing. Check seasoning and serve.

Variations
1 Add other salad greens in season – Cos lettuce, endive, chicory, batavia, young lettuce leaves, watercress and French mâche (lamb's lettuce or corn salad).

2 Add finely chopped garlic and shallots to salad dressing.

3 Add orange segments and curry powder to salad dressing.

4 Add crumbled Roquefort cheese and chopped walnuts to salad dressing.

5 Add chopped peanuts, soy sauce and a dash of Tabasco to salad dressing.

6 Add 1 teaspoon each mayonnaise and double cream to salad dressing and sprinkle generously with fresh chives and fennel.

7 For crunch appeal, add diced celery, green pepper or fennel.

To make a well-flavoured vinaigrette dressing: in a small bowl, blend 2 tablespoons wine vinegar (or 1 tablespoon each balsamic vinegar and lime juice) with 1 level teaspoon Dijon mustard. Mix well, then add 6-8 tablespoons extra virgin olive oil and whisk with a fork until dressing is well mixed. Season generously with coarse sea salt, freshly ground pepper and crushed dried chillies, to taste.

Italian Tomato Salad

Leaping Hare Salad of Goat's Cheese and Roasted Peppers

Eighteenth-century Dressing

1 small boiled potato, peeled
2 anchovy fillets
2 hard-boiled egg yolks
1 teaspoon Dijon mustard

2 tablespoons wine vinegar
6 tablespoons olive oil
1-2 tablespoons finely chopped onion
Salt and freshly ground pepper

1 Pound boiled potato, anchovy fillets and hard-boiled egg yolks through a fine sieve into a bowl.

2 In a small bowl, stir Dijon mustard into wine vinegar until well blended. Add olive oil, finely chopped onion and salt and freshly ground pepper, to taste.

3 Pour over sieved ingredients and mix well. Add to Tossed Green Salad (see page 179) and toss well.

Italian Tomato Salad

SERVES 4-6

8-12 whole small tomatoes
1 head Cos lettuce
2 tablespoons wine vinegar
½ teaspoon dry mustard
6 tablespoons olive oil

1 clove garlic, finely chopped
2 tablespoons finely chopped
parsley
1 teaspoon dried oregano
Salt and freshly ground pepper

1 Peel tomatoes.

2 Wash Cos lettuce, discarding any yellowed or damaged leaves, and cut leaves into 3.5cm/1½-inch strips. Shake dry and chill.

3 Prepare Italian dressing by combining wine vinegar, dry mustard and olive oil in a small bowl and mix well. Add garlic, parsley, dried oregano, and salt and freshly ground pepper to taste.

4 When ready to serve, arrange peeled whole tomatoes and lettuce strips in a salad bowl. Pour over dressing and toss well before serving.

Note: If tomatoes are too large, cut in half. Cherry tomatoes are too small.

Leaping Hare Salad of Goat's Cheese and Roasted Peppers

SERVES 4

4 crottin goat's cheese (refrigerated for 1 hour minimum)
2 red peppers
2 yellow peppers
16 cherry tomatoes
2 cloves garlic, cut into thin strips

4 tablespoons olive oil
Sea salt
Freshly ground pepper

Garnish:
Rocket

1 Cut the peppers in quarters, lengthways; remove the stem and seeds and slice off any fleshy pith.

2 Lay peppers in a roasting tray, cut side up. Put a cherry tomato in each quarter and sprinkle with thin strips of garlic. Drizzle with olive oil and season with salt and freshly ground pepper.

3 Roast in a preheated oven (425°F/220°C/Gas 7) for 20-25 minutes until slightly coloured. Five minutes before the peppers are ready, preheat grill on full power.

4 When the grill is hot, put the crottins on a baking tray, brush the tops lightly with oil and grill for approximately 2-3 minutes until browned but still retaining their shape.

5 Place 4 quarters of a pepper on each plate with a grilled crottin in the centre. Drizzle with olive oil and serve immediately.

Cucumber Salad with Fresh Herbs

SERVES 4-6

1 large cucumber
Salt and freshly ground pepper
2 tablespoons wine vinegar
1 tablespoon Dijon mustard
6 tablespoons olive oil

2 tablespoons finely chopped
* tarragon*
1 tablespoon finely chopped chives
4-6 tablespoons double cream

1 Peel and slice cucumber thinly (use a mandolin cutter if you have one). Place cucumber slices in a glass bowl and toss with salt and freshly ground pepper to taste.

2 Prepare a dressing by beating half the wine vinegar and half the Dijon mustard together until well mixed. Add half the olive oil and salt and freshly ground pepper to taste, and beat again until they form an emulsion. Pour over cucumber slices and toss. Chill for at least 30 minutes. Drain juices from cucumbers.

3 Make a second vinaigrette dressing with remaining wine vinegar, Dijon mustard and olive oil. Season to taste with tarragon and chives. Pour dressing over salad and toss well.

4 Whip double cream until stiff. Add salt to taste and spoon over salad.

Mediterranean Fruit Salad

Japanese Salad

SERVES 4-6

1 head lettuce
1 bunch watercress
1 bunch radishes, thinly sliced
1 clove garlic, finely chopped
1 spring onion, thinly sliced

Shoyu Dressing
2 tablespoons wine vinegar
2 tablespoons soy sauce
Dry mustard
6-8 tablespoons olive oil
Freshly ground pepper

1 Wash and trim lettuce and watercress. Dry thoroughly. Trim radishes and slice paper-thin. Chill.

2 Assemble salad by arranging lettuce leaves in a salad bowl, spreading watercress on top and scattering sliced radishes over.

3 Make shoyu dressing by combining wine vinegar, soy sauce and mustard in a small bowl. Add olive oil, and freshly ground pepper to taste.

4 Just before serving pour the dressing over the salad and sprinkle with finely chopped garlic and thinly sliced spring onion. Toss until every ingredient glistens.

Mediterranean Fruit Salad

SERVES 6-8

6-8 oranges
450g/1 lb strawberries
450g/1 lb white grapes
Ripe olives
Fresh mint

Honey and Lemon Dressing
1 tablespoon honey
2 tablespoons lemon juice
6 tablespoons olive oil
Salt and freshly ground pepper
Crushed dried chillies

1 Peel oranges, removing all white pith, and slice into rings. Wash and hull strawberries. Wash grapes and remove stems. Combine fruits in a serving dish and chill.

2 Prepare honey and lemon dressing by stirring honey into lemon juice and adding olive oil and salt, freshly ground pepper and crushed dried chillies, to taste.

3 Just before serving, garnish fruits with ripe olives and a few sprigs of fresh mint and pour over honey and lemon dressing.

Note: This Mediterranean salad dressing is excellent with sliced fresh fruits, or a combination of fruit and green salad, or with thickly sliced cucumbers and coarsely chopped mint.

Lavender and Honey Ice Cream

Pears in Brouilly

Desserts

A very good dinner deserves a happy ending. Something just that much more exciting than a salad of fresh fruits (even when doused with champagne) or a fresh fruit sorbet topped with puréed raspberries (*à la Cardinale*) or blackcurrants (*au cassis*). Yet, a dessert need not be elaborate or difficult to make to be memorable. I often serve a large, piping hot open tart of thinly sliced fresh fruit (apples, pears, peaches or pineapples) brushed with dark rum and melted butter, accompanied by mounds of chilled whipped cream or crème fraîche, or little chocolate 'pots' topped with a float of orange-flavoured curaçao or Tia Maria.

For more festive occasions, I like to make the edible tulip-shaped pastry cases taught to me many years ago by René Lasserre, whose elegant restaurant *Chez Lasserre* is located just off the Champs Elysées in Paris. '*Tulipe glacée Lasserre*' combines 125g/5 oz each flour and icing sugar with 3 egg whites and 2 egg yolks. This creamy butter is spread thinly in a saucer-sized circle on a baking sheet, baked for 5-6 minutes only in a preheated moderate oven (180°C/350°F/Gas 4) and pressed (while still hot) over an orange to form a round-bottomed tulip-shaped cup. *Chez Lasserre* fills the cup with vanilla ice cream, fresh fruits and a liqueur-flavoured syrup and caps the whole confection with a gossamer-light froth of spun sugar. My favourite version is simpler: no spun sugar, just a decorative swirl of whipped cream to finish it off and a delicious circle of macadamia nut brittle ice cream, studded with glacéed chestnuts, in a dark rum-flavoured syrup. Try it.

I find that top French restaurants often make a speciality of delicious desserts and puddings that look and sound far more complicated than they actually are. I have chosen a series of favourite desserts that are perfect for a special dinner party, because most of the preparatory work can be completed the day before, leaving just the finishing touches for the last minute.

Summer Apple Charlotte, a French baked pudding served with wine-glazed apples and chilled whipped cream is one of the few exceptions. The pudding (see page 199) can indeed be prepared the day before the party, but it must be baked for 45 minutes before guests arrive and then kept warm in the lowest of ovens until time to serve.

Cold Praline Soufflé

SERVES 4-6

25g/1 oz powdered gelatine
300ml/½ pint milk
4 egg yolks
100g/4 oz castor sugar
1-2 tablespoons instant coffee
50g/2 oz semi-sweet chocolate,
  melted
300 ml/½ pint double cream,
  whipped

100g/4oz sugar
2 tablespoons water
100g/4oz chopped almonds
4 egg whites, stiffly beaten

Decoration
Grated chocolate or powdered coffee
Whipped cream
Chocolate bâtons

1 Soak gelatine in a little cold water until soft.

2 In a mixing bowl, combine the egg yolks, sugar, instant coffee and melted chocolate. Heat milk to boiling point in a small saucepan and add to the egg and mocha mixture, whisking constantly until well blended.

3 Place mixture in the top of a double saucepan and cook over water, stirring constantly, until mixture coats the back of a spoon. Strain if necessary. Whisk in gelatine. Pour into a bowl and allow to cool. Then stir over ice until the mixture begins to set.

4 Fold in the praline mixture (see below), then fold in the whipped cream and then the stiffly beaten egg whites. Pour into a prepared 15-16 cm/6-7 inch soufflé dish, edged with a standing collar of greaseproof paper 5-8 cm/2-3 inches above the rim of the dish. Refrigerate to set.

5 Remove band of paper, coat sides of soufflé with grated chocolate or powdered coffee and decorate top with piped cream and chocolate bâtons.

6 To make the praline: Put 100g/4oz sugar, 2 tablespoons water in a small, heavy bottomed saucepan and heat, stirring continuously, until the sugar has dissolved. Bring to the boil and boil for 5 minutes or until the sugar has slightly caramalised. Remove the pan from the heat, stir in 100g/40z chopped almonds and pour onto an oiled baking tray. Leave until cold and hard, then crush the praline with a rolling pin to a coarse powder.

Rice à la Royale

SERVES 8

150g/6 oz pudding rice
6 tablespoons granulated sugar
600ml/1 pint milk
20g/¾ oz powdered gelatine
600ml/1 pint home-made custard
1-1½ teaspoons vanilla essence
150g/6 oz mixed glacéed fruits,
  diced
6 tablespoons double cream
3-4 tablespoons Kirsch

To decorate:
3-4 small ripe dessert pears, halved,
  cored and poached in light syrup or
  brushed with lemon juice.
Glacé cherries, halved
Clusters of seedless grapes
Ripe plums, halved
Canned apricot halves

To cook Rice:
1 Put (unwashed) rice in a heavy, medium-sized saucepan. Cover with cold water to come 2 inches above rice. Bring to the boil: dislodge any grains stuck to the pan and simmer for 5 minutes.

2 Drain rice thoroughly in a colander. Return to the pan. Add granulated sugar and milk. Bring to simmering point, stirring frequently, and simmering gently, uncovered until rice is soft and most of the milk has been absorbed, about 20 minutes. Remove pan from heat: Cover and allow to cool.

To assemble Dish:
3 Sprinkle gelatine over 4 or 5 tablespoons cold water in a cup and leave to soften.

4 Place cup containing gelatine in a bowl of hot water and stir until gelatine has completely dissolved. Beat gelatine into home-made custard and flavour to taste with vanilla essence.

5 Stir diced glacé fruits and cream into custard mixture and add cooked rice. Add Kirsch, to taste.

6 Pour mixture into a deep, round, 1.5 litre/3 pint mould, or two smaller moulds and chill until firmly set, preferably overnight, to make sure rice mixture is firm enough to cut into slices (or wedges) when serving. To unmould rice: Dip mould (or moulds) for just one or two seconds into very hot water. Place a large serving dish on top. Invert and gently shake rice mould(s) out on to dish. Decorate with halved and cored pears which you have poached in a light syrup (or, if they are really ripe and soft, simply brushed all over with lemon juice to prevent discoloration), halved glacé cherries, apricots, clusters of seedless grapes and plums and serve very cold.

Lavender and Honey Ice cream

SERVES 4

500ml/ ¾ pint milk
5 tablespoons lavender honey
130 ml/ 4 fl oz double cream

100g/ 4 oz caster sugar
1 vanilla pod
5 egg yolks

1 In a medium-sized saucepan, combine the milk, honey, double cream, vanilla pod and half the sugar and bring gently to the boil, stirring constantly, until the sugar has completely melted.

2 In the meantime, in a small bowl, beat the egg yolks with the remaining sugar until they are light coloured and foamy.

3 Strain the boiling milk mixture over the eggs and stir over hot but not boiling water until smooth and thick. Strain into a bowl and bring rapidly to room temperature.

4 When cold, pour the mixture into the ice cream maker and freeze according to manufacturer's instructions.

* If no lavender honey is available, add a sprig or two of dried lavender to egg and honey mixture and cook as above.

Pears in Brouilly

SERVES 4

1.25g/2 ½ lb small pears, peeled
225g/8 oz sugar
Peel of 1 orange
1 stick cinnamon

2 cloves
Brouilly (or other good Beaujolais wine)
Whipped cream or crème fraîche

1 Put peeled pears in a saucepan with the sugar, 150 ml/¼ pint water, orange peel, cinnamon and cloves. Simmer, covered, for about 15 minutes. Add 300 ml/½ pint Brouilly, a quality red wine from the Beaujolais region of France, and continue to cook, uncovered, over a low heat for 15 minutes, or until pears are tender but have not lost their shape.

2 Remove pears from the saucepan and carefully transfer them to a medium-sized bowl. Reduce syrup over a high heat to half its original quantity. Cool.

3 When reserved syrup is cool, add 4 tablespoons Brouilly and pour over pears. Chill in the refrigerator.

4 Serve pears very cold with whipped cream or crème fraîche.

Ananas Givrée

SERVES 4-6

2-3 well-ripened small pineapples
2-3 tablespoons dark rum
2-3 tablespoons icing sugar

600 ml/1 pint pineapple water ice,
  or sherbet
Small fresh flowers, or sliced fresh fruits

1 Cut pineapples in half vertically, slicing straight through the leaves, to make 4-6 'boats'.

2 With a small sharp knife cut out the pineapple flesh, taking care not to pierce the skin. Slice pineapple flesh, discard cores and dice flesh into a bowl. Add dark rum and icing sugar. Chill diced pineapple and pineapple shells for 2 hours.

3 When ready to serve, drain diced pineapple and spoon into the shells. Top each shell with a scoop of pineapple water ice (or sherbet). Decorate leaves of pineapple with 3 or 4 fresh flowers (or sliced fresh fruits) and serve at once.

Crème Caramel à l'Orange

SERVES 4-6

300 ml/½ pint milk
150ml/¼ pint single cream
Strip of orange peel
A piece of vanilla pod, split
50g/2 oz castor sugar
3 eggs, beaten
1 egg yolk, beaten

4 tablespoons orange juice
½ teaspoon vanilla essence

Caramel
100g/4 oz granulated sugar
1-2 tablespoons water

1 Preheat oven to 180°C/350°F/Gas 4.

2 Combine milk and cream in a pan with orange peel, vanilla pod and castor sugar, and bring to the boil. Remove pan from heat; cover and leave to infuse for 5-10 minutes.

3 Remove orange peel and vanilla pod from milk. Stir milk mixture into beaten eggs and egg yolk - do not beat it in (this, together with a too-hot oven, is what usually causes air bubbles). Flavour with orange juice and vanilla essence.

4 To prepare caramel: Select a straight-sided, 900ml/1 pint metal mould. Add granulated sugar and 1-2 tablespoons water, and swirl pan over a low heat until dissolved. Raise heat and boil rapidly, without stirring, until syrup turns into a rich, dark caramel. Watch it like a hawk, drawing the caramel away from the heat before it is quite ready (it carries on cooking from the heat of the mould and will burn at the slightest provocation).

5 Holding handles of mould in a thick cloth, swirl caramel around with great care so that bottom and sides of mould are well coated. Cool slightly.

6 Pour in egg mixture; cover mould with a piece of foil and stand it in a roasting tin. Pour in hot water to come halfway up sides of mould; place roasting tin over a medium heat until the water just begins to bubble.

7 Transfer to the oven and immediately reduce temperature to 170°C/325°F/Gas 3. Bake custard for 35-40 minutes, or until set.

8 Cool mould, then turn out carefully on to a deepish serving dish to catch the caramel syrup.

Compôte of Berries in Red Wine

SERVES 4-6

6 tablespoons sugar
1 stick cinnamon
Peel of 1 orange
150ml/¼ pint red Burgundy
1 punnet redcurrants

1 punnet strawberries
1 punnet raspberries
1 punnet blueberries
Whipped cream or crème fraîche

1 Combine 150ml/¼ pint water, sugar, cinnamon stick and strips of ½ the orange peel in a saucepan. Bring to the boil and cook until the sugar dissolves, stirring constantly. Add the wine and continue to cook until sauce comes to the boil again. Remove from heat. Cool.

2 Wash and hull or stem redcurrants, strawberries, raspberries and blueberries, discarding any fruits that are not perfect.

3 Combine prepared fruits in a glass serving bowl. Pour the cooled Burgundy syrup over fruit and chill for several hours before serving.

4 Just before serving, cut thin julienne strips of remaining ½ orange; sprinkle over berry compôte. Serve with whipped cream or crème fraîche.

Summer Apple Charlotte

SERVES 6

8 eating apples
2 bananas, chopped
4 pineapple slices, chopped
150g/6 oz butter
1 teaspoon grated orange rind

Juice of ½ lemon
Sugar
2 tablespoons apricot jam
1 loaf sliced white bread
Chilled whipped cream

1 Peel and core apples and chop coarsely. Add chopped bananas and pineapple. Cook chopped fruit in 50g/2 oz butter with orange rind and lemon juice, covered, for about 10 minutes, or until fruit is soft. Remove cover and cook, stirring continuously to prevent scorching, until mixture is quite dry. Sweeten to taste with sugar and apricot jam.

2 Butter bottom and sides of a 15cm/6 inch charlotte or soufflé mould and dust with sugar.

3 Trim crusts from sliced bread; cut enough triangles to cover bottom of mould.

4 Clarify remaining butter. Dip triangles one by one in butter and line bottom of mould, overlapping the triangles to make an attractive pattern. Line the sides of the mould with strips of bread dipped in clarified butter, also overlapping. Fill the mould with the fruit mixture and cover with triangles of butter-dipped bread. Cover with buttered paper and bake in the oven (190°C/375°F/Gas 5) for 45 minutes, or until the bread is golden. Let the mould stand for 5-10 minutes after removing from oven.

5 To serve, invert the charlotte on a heated serving dish. Surround with peeled, cored and halved apples which you have poached in a red or white wine syrup (see Pears in Brouilly, page 195). Serve with chilled whipped cream.

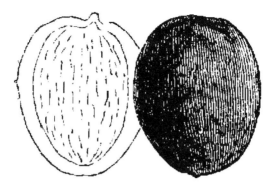

Frozen Almond Creams

SERVES 6-8

300ml/½ pint double cream
2 egg whites
Castor sugar

Salt
100g/4 oz chopped toasted almonds
Sherry, Marsala or Cognac

1 Whip cream.

2 Beat egg whites, add sugar and salt, to taste, and continue beating until mixture is stiff and glossy.

3 Fold chopped almonds (reserving 2 level tablespoons for garnish) into egg mixture with whipped cream. Stir in sherry, Marsala or Cognac to taste, and spoon mixture into 6 or 8 individual soufflé dishes or custard cups. Sprinkle with reserved almonds and freeze for 4 hours.

Caribbean Fruit Salad

SERVES 4

4 passion fruits
2 small ripe mangoes, peeled and
    sliced
150g/8oz blueberries
100g/4oz raspberries
50g/2oz loganberries (optional)

Juice and grated zest of 1 lime
Juice of 1 orange
2 tablespoons sugar
2-4 tablespoons dark Jamaican rum
5 sprigs fresh mint

1 To prepare fruits: Cut the passion fruits in half. Using a teaspoon, scoop out the flesh into a small sieve placed over a bowl. Using a wooden spoon, rub the flesh through the sieve, discarding the seeds.

2 Combine the flesh with the sliced mangoes and the berries. Sprinkle with the juice and zest of the lime and orange juice and sugar to taste. Then stir in the rum and toss fruits to mix the flavours of the dressing.

3 Cut the leaves of 1 sprig of mint into thin slivers and scatter over the salad.

4 Chill the salad in the refrigerator for at least 2 hours before serving. When ready to serve, spoon sliced fruits and berries on to 4 chilled dessert plates; garnish each plate with a sprig of mint and serve immediately.

Coffee Granita

SERVES 6

300ml/10floz fresh, hot, strong
   coffee
75-100g/4oz castor sugar
6 ice cubes
150ml/5floz whipping cream, whipped
Poached fruits for decoration

Syrup
185 ml/7 fl oz water
185g/7 oz castor sugar
6 fresh mint leaves (optional)

1 If using the freezer in your refrigerator, turn it down to its lowest temperature (the highest setting) about 1 hour before you start.

2 Add sugar to hot coffee and stir until dissolved. Then add ice cubes to the coffee and stir until ice has melted.

3 Pour the mixture into a large flat dish or container and put it in the freezer or freezing compartment of the refrigerator.During the course of the day, fork over the solidifying liquid regularly, scraping the crystals from the edges of the dish into the still-liquid central part. Continue until the whole is set into a mass of small light crystals.

4 Fill 6 claret or sherbert glasses with the granita, shaping it into a dome-shape with a spoon.

5 Top each serving with whipped cream and a sprig of fresh mint. Serve immediately.

Clafoutis of Red Fruits

350g/½ lb fresh plums
225g/½ lb fresh black cherries
6 tablespoons water, wine or juice
   from canned cherries (if you are
   using canned fruit)
125g/5 oz sugar

Rich Custard Mixture
3 tablespoons softened butter
175g/6 oz cream cheese, at room
   temperature

300ml/½ pint double cream
2 eggs
4 tablespoons flour
Grated zest of 1 orange
Butter
2 tablespoons Kirsch

Garnish
Icing sugar
Fresh raspberries
Sprigs of fresh mint

1 Wash plums, halve them and remove stones. Wash and pit cherries. Place red fruits in a saucepan with water, wine (or juice from canned cherries) and 4 tablespoons of the sugar and cook over a medium heat for 20 minutes, stirring occasionally, or until fruits reduce to a compote. Note: Add a little more water (or juice from canned cherries) from time to time if necessary.

2 To make Rich Custard Mixture: blend the 3 tablespoons softened butter with the cream cheese and the double cream until smooth. Then beat in the eggs with the remaining sugar and flour and grated orange rind.

3 Butter the baking dish. Spread half of the custard mixture in the bottom of the dish. Spoon over the stewed fruits; sprinkle with Kirsch then top with remaining custard.

4 Sprinkle clafoutis with icing sugar and bake in a preheated oven (180°C/350°F/Mark 4) for 30 minutes, or until the custard is just set and its surface is lightly golden. Decorate with raspberries and sprigs of fresh mint.

Bread and Butter Pudding with Orange and Kumquats

SERVES 6

100-150g/ 4-6oz softened butter
10-12 slices brioche bread
Juice and finely grated rind of 2
oranges and 1lemon
75g/ 3oz castor sugar
6 kumquats, cut into a fine julienne.

Custard:
450ml/¾ pint milk
2 eggs
2 level tablespoons castor sugar
25g/ 1oz seedless raisins (optional)
4 tablespoons lightly whipped cream

1 Preheat oven to 200°C/400°F/ Gas 6. Then grease a shallow, 3 pint baking dish generously with some of the butter,

2 Remove crusts from brioche bread. Spread slices with butter and cut into small cannulated round shapes with cookie cutters.

3 Combine juice and finely grated rinds of oranges and lemon in a bowl. Add castor sugar and stir until melted.

4 Soak each brioche shape in orange syrup one by one and arrange them, buttered side up, in overlapping rows in the prepared baking dish.

5 To make custard: Heat milk to just below boiling point. Beat eggs lightly in a bowl and pour hot milk on to them gradually, beating constantly. Return mixture to the pan; add sugar and raisins if used, and stir over a low heat until the custard thickens enough to coat the back of a spoon. (Take great care not to let custard boil, or eggs will curdle. Use a double saucepan for this if you have one.) Remove custard from heat; cool slightly and stir in cream.

6 Pour custard over brioche shapes in the baking dish. Soak julienne of kumquats in left-over orange syrup for a few minutes. Sprinkle over pudding and bake for 30 minutes, or until crisp and golden on the outside, with a soft, creamy centre.

Italian Baked Peaches en Papillote

SERVES 6

4 large firm peaches
4 tablespoons Mascarpone cheese
4 teaspoons icing sugar
5-6 tablespoons crushed macaroons
3 tablespoons ground almonds

2-3 teaspoons finely chopped candied
* orange peel*
1 egg white
6 tablespoons Marsala
Chilled whipped cream

1 Preheat oven to 180°C/350°F/Gas 4.

2 To peel peaches, place them in a sieve over a bowl one or two at a time, and pour over boiling water to loosen skins. Then, holding peach in a cloth, peel off skin with your fingers.

3 Cut peaches in half and remove stones. Arrange peach halves, cut sides up, side by side on a baking tray.

4 In a bowl, work Mascarpone cheese with a wooden spoon until soft. Sift in icing sugar, beat until creamy, then stir in crushed macaroons, ground almonds and chopped candied orange peel.

5 Beat egg white until stiff but not dry and fold lightly into macaroon mixture with a metal spoon.

6 Pile macaroon mixture into the cavity of each peach, mounding it up attractively.

7 Place stuffed peaches in parchment paper ovals (as in *en papillotte* recipes, see pages 143-150), crimp edges together and bake for 20 minutes in a preheated oven until soft but not mushy.

8 Serve peaches hot with some of the Marsala flavoured juices poured over them, accompanied by chilled whipped cream.

Tips: If you have no icing sugar, place castor sugar or granulated sugar in a liquidiser and blend until reduced to a powder.
The sugar deposit which has to be removed before chopping candied peel is excellent for sweetening stewed apples.

Apple Beignets

SERVES 4

4 Granny Smiths, Worcester Pearmain or Cox's Orange Pippin apples	**Beignet batter:**
	125g/5 oz flour
	1 egg, beaten
Juice of 2 lemons	2 tablespoons light cooking oil
Sugar	150ml/5 fl oz lager
Oil for deep frying	1-2 tablespoons brandy
	150ml/½ pint water
	2 egg whites
	Salt

To make Beignet batter
1 Sift the flour into a large mixing bowl and make a well in the centre. Gradually add beaten egg, oil, lager, brandy and 150ml/½ pint water. Whisk the mixture constantly to make a smooth batter. *Note:* Be careful not to work the batter too much, or it will become too elastic, and therefore produce tough beignets.

2 Cover batter mixture and leave to rest in the refrigerator for at least two hours.

3 In a bowl whisk egg whites with a pinch of salt to stiff peaks, and fold into chilled batter mixture. Use immediately.

To prepare apples:
4 Peel and core apples, slice thickly and place in bowl. Add lemon juice, to cover.

To fry apple beignets:
5 Dip lemon-marinated apple slices one by one in batter, lifting each one out with your fingers, or with a skewer, and dropping it into deep fryer of boiling oil.

6 Fry beignets turning them from time to time, until golden brown on all sides. Lift beignets out with a skewer or slotted spoon and dry on sugared paper in a moderate oven. Continue until all are cooked. Serve with additional sugar and lemon wedges.

Cakes

There is no branch of cooking where greater care and accuracy are required than in cake-making. If you are new to baking I recommend strongly that you follow cake recipes carefully, without altering quantities or cooking times, until you have made the recipe at least twice. Then experiment as you like.

The handling of the cake has much to do with its lightness. Some cooks seem to have a knack of turning out light cakes and pastry, while others have to practise before their creations are a success.

Always preheat your oven before making your cake, especially for cakes which include baking powder. They will spoil if they have to stand waiting for the oven to heat, even more so if they are put into an oven that is not hot enough. You will find a moderate oven is best for most cakes; rather hotter for small and light cakes than for thicker fruit cakes.

Assemble all ingredients and cake tins before you start to make the cake. If fruit is included in the recipe, prepare it in advance.

In some cake mixtures (especially the plainer ones) the butter or fat is rubbed into the flour; in others, it is beaten to a cream before the other ingredients are mixed with it, or the eggs or egg yolks are creamed with the sugar, and the butter added in a melted form. And in some sponges no fat at all is used.

1 When a cake rises in a cone in the centre, this indicates that your oven was too hot when you started baking. As a result, the sides of the cake hardened with a crust before the mixture had time to rise.

2 If the cake rises at one side, your oven is hotter one side than the other. Correct this by turning the cake from time to time during baking.

3 Do not open the oven door for at least 5 minutes after the cake has been put in, and then only with the greatest care. Do not slam the oven door; it can be fatal to the successful rising of the cake. Handle a cake carefully during baking. Moving or shaking it during baking is almost certain to cause it to fall.

4 Be sure the cake is sufficiently cooked before removing it from the oven. Small cakes are ready if they feel firm when gently touched with the finger. Larger cakes should be tested by running a warm skewer into the centre. If the skewer comes out sticky, the cake is not cooked enough; if dry, the baking is finished.

5 Allow cakes to stand for a minute or two before removing them from the cake tins (they will turn out more easily).

6 Always cool cakes on a wire cake rack so that the air gets round the bottom and sides.

Sponge Cake

MAKES 6 PORTIONS

100g/4 oz butter
100g/4 oz plain flour
1 teaspoon baking powder
100g/4 oz castor sugar

Few drops vanilla essence or finely
 grated lemon rind
2 eggs
Red cherry jam
Icing sugar

1 Preheat oven to 190°C/375°F/Gas 5.

2 Brush two 17 cm/7 inch sandwich tins with melted butter. Line bases with circles of greaseproof paper and brush these with melted butter.

3 In a large bowl, cream 100g/4 oz butter, castor sugar and flavouring together until light and fluffy.

4 In another, smaller bowl, whisk eggs until frothy. Add to creamed mixture a few tablespoons at a time, beating well between each addition.

5 Sift flour with baking powder, and resift over creamed mixture. Fold in lightly with a spatula.

6 Divide batter evenly between prepared tins and level off tops.

7 Bake layers (on the same shelf if possible) for 25 minutes, or until they are a rich golden colour on top, have shrunk slightly from sides of tins and spring back when pressed lightly.

8 Turn layers out on to a folded cloth and peel off base papers. Turn right side up again and cool on wire rack.

9 When layers are quite cold, sandwich with good red cherry jam, warmed to make it spread more easily, and dust with icing sugar.

Genoese Sponge

MAKES TWO 17–20 CM/ 7½–8 INCH LAYERS

75g/3 oz plain flour
25g/1oz cornflour
125 g/5oz unsalted butter
4 eggs

100g/4 oz castor sugar
1 teaspoon vanilla essence or finely grated
  rind of ½ lemon

Excellent for layer cakes, iced cakes and petits fours.

1 Preheat oven to 180°C/350°F/Gas 4. Sift flour with cornflour three times.

2 Take the bowl in which you intend to whisk up the cake and select a large sauce-pan over which it will fit firmly. Pour 5 cm/2 inches water into the pan and bring to the boil.

3 Place about 125g/5 oz unsalted butter in another, smaller pan and lower the pan into the heating water so that the butter melts without sizzling or bubbling. Remove pan from water. Brush two 17-20 cm/7½- 8 inch sandwich tins with a little melted butter. Line bases with greaseproof paper and brush again with butter.

4 Combine eggs, castor sugar and vanilla essence or grated lemon rind in the bowl. Set it over barely simmering water and whisk vigorously until very thick, light and lukewarm. Remove bowl from heat. Stand bowl on a cool surface and continue to whisk until mixture leaves a distinct trail on the surface when beaters are lifted (3-5 minutes if beating with an electric mixer at high speed).

5 Gradually resift flour mixture over surface, folding it in lightly but thoroughly with a large metal spoon or spatula. Add 8 tablespoons melted butter and continue with the folding motion until it has been completely absorbed. This may take slightly longer than you expect, so work as you can to avoid deflating the mixture.

6 Divide batter evenly between prepared tins. Bake for 15-20 minutes, or until cakes are well risen, golden brown on top and springy to the touch.

7 Turn out onto wire racks. Peel off lining paper and allow cakes to cool completely before using.

Almond and Hazelnut Gâteau

225g/8 oz almonds
125g/5 oz hazelnuts
225g/8 oz granulated sugar
8 egg whites
Butter
Castor sugar
Chocolate paillettes

Chocolate Cream
6 tablespoons cold butter
2 tablespoons castor sugar
150 ml/¼ pint cold crème pâtissière
 (see page 220)

Unsweetened baking chocolate, melted
 and cooked

Praline Cream
Blanched almonds
Castor sugar
Vanilla essence
6 tablespoons cold butter
150ml/¼ pint cold crème pâtissière (see
 page 220)
Powdered praline

1 Grill almonds and hazelnuts separately in 2 trays: remove husks by rubbing in metal strainer. Combine nuts in an electric blender or a mortar, and crush very finely. Add granulated sugar and mix well.

2 Beat egg whites until they form peaks and mix with nut mixture (without letting eggs fall). Spoon mixture into 4 well-buttered, shallow, rectangular cake tins and bake in a preheated oven (180°C/350°F/Gas 4). Allow to cool.

3 To assemble cake: Put one layer on a flat serving dish and spread with chocolate cream. Top with another layer and spread thickly with prâline cream. Top with another layer and spread with chocolate cream. Top with final layer. Smooth sides, sprinkle top of cake with castor sugar and sides with chocolate pailettes. Keep for 24 hours before serving.

4 To make chocolate cream: Cream cold butter well with sugar, then blend this thoroughly and slowly with cold *crème pâtissière* , added little by little. Stir in melted and cooled unsweetened baking chocolate, to taste.

5 To make praline cream: Mix equal quantities of blanched almonds and sugar, and heat mixture in a thick-bottomed frying pan until well caramelized, stirring to brown it evenly. Add a few drops vanilla essence. Cool on a baking tray until it hardens. Crush to a powder by chopping and pounding with a heavy rolling pin. Cream cold butter well with 1 tablespoon castor sugar, then blend this thoroughly and slowly with cold *crème pâtissière* added little by little. Stir in powdered praline, to taste.

Chocolate Almond Cake

125g/5 oz almonds, skin on
Softened butter
100g/4 oz semi-sweet chocolate
100g/4 oz butter
125g/5 oz sugar
3 eggs
Grated rind of 1 large orange
4 tablespoons fine dry
  breadcrumbs

Chocolate Icing
150g/6 oz unsweetened or plain
  chocolate
8 tablespoons double cream
50g/2 oz sugar
50g/2oz butter
450g/1 lb icing sugar, sieved

1 Grind the almonds in electric blender or food processor. They should be as fine as possible.

2 Preheat oven to 190°C/375°F/Gas 5.

3 Butter the sides of a 20 cm/8 inch round cake tin with a little softened butter. Line the bottom with greaseproof paper.

4 Melt the chocolate in the top of a double saucepan over hot (not boiling) water. Remove from heat. Reserve. Work 100g/4 oz diced butter with an electric beater until soft and light-coloured. Gradually beat in the sugar. Then add the eggs one at a time, beating until each egg is thoroughly assimilated into the mixture. Mixture might look curdled at this point. Don't worry.

5 Stir in the melted chocolate, ground almonds, orange rind and breadcrumbs. Pour mixture into the prepared cake tin and bake in the preheated oven for 25 minutes.

6 Remove cake from oven, invert tin and allow cake to cool on a cake rack for 30 minutes. Remove cake from tin, strip off kitchen paper and cool cake. Leave cake overnight.

7 The following day, slice cake carefully into 2 or 3 layers. The centre of the cake should still be a little moist and soft.

8 To make chocolate icing: Melt chocolate in cream with butter over hot water in a double saucepan. When smooth, add sieved icing sugar. Mix well.

9 Cool slightly before using to spread between cake layers and over top and sides of the cake.

Little Summer Fruit Towers

SERVES 6

Sponge
Butter
3 eggs
75g/3 oz castor sugar
75g/3 oz plain flour, sifted

Strawberry Bavaroise Filling
24-30 strawberries, mashed
Finely grated rind of 1 orange
150 ml/¼ pint milk
1 egg yolk
2 tablespoons castor sugar
1 teaspoon powdered gelatine
150 ml/¼ pint double cream
2 tablespoons Grand Marnier or

Cointreau
Red food colouring
2 egg whites

Raspberry Cream
300 ml/½ pint double cream
¼ teaspoon vanilla essence
1 punnet raspberries
Powdered sugar
Lemon juice or framboise liqueur

Decoration
Whipped cream and ripe raspberries or
strawberries

1 Preheat oven to 180°C/350°F/Gas 4.

2 Butter a 30 x 20 cm/12 x 8-inch swiss roll tin and line with buttered greaseproof paper.

3 To make sponge: Whisk eggs and sugar over hot water until mixture leaves a trail on the surface. Remove from heat and fold in flour with a metal spoon. Pour into prepared tin. Bake for 15-20 minutes, or until sponge is golden and springy. Turn out on to a wire rack; peel off lining paper. Cool.

4 To make strawberry bavaroise filling: Combine orange rind and milk and bring to the boil, stirring constantly. Remove from heat. Whisk egg yolk with half the castor sugar, then gradually whisk in hot milk. Sprinkle gelatine over 2 tablespoons cold water in a cup and leave for 10 minutes. Place cup in a bowl of hot water and stir until gelatine has completely dissolved. Blend thoroughly with milk and egg mixture. Whip cream lightly and fold into strawberry mixture. Add Grand Marnier or Cointreau, and a little red food colouring to tint mixture a rich pink. Fold in mashed strawberries. Whisk egg whites until stiff, add remaining castor sugar and continue to whisk until stiff and glossy. Fold into strawberry mixture.

5 To line six 150 ml/¼-pint turret moulds with sponge: Carefully slice sponge cake into 2 thin layers 0.5 cm/¼ inch thick, using a serrated knife. Cut a circle of sponge to fit the bottom of each mould. Then cut a strip to fit completely round inside of each mould, trimming ends so there is no overlap.

6 Fill sponge-lined moulds with strawberry mixture and chill until firmly set.

7 To make raspberry cream: Whip cream until stiff, then beat in vanilla essence. Purée raspberries with a little powdered sugar and lemon juice, or framboise liqueur, to taste. Add to whipped cream and whisk until thoroughly blended.

8 When ready to serve, turn strawberry towers out on to a wire rack over a flat dish. Mask each tower completely with raspberry cream and transfer to individual serving dishes. Top each tower with a swirl of whipped cream and garnish with a ripe raspberry or strawberry.

Orange Layer Cake

Cake
6 eggs, separated
150g/6 oz sugar
2 tablespoons water
Grated rind of 1 orange
Generous pinch of salt
75g/3 oz flour

25g/1 oz cornflour
Butter and flour for cake tin
Orange topping

Decoration
Peeled orange segments or chocolate
  curls

1 To make cake: Beat egg yolks, sugar, water, orange rind and salt until light and fluffy (5 minutes in mixer at high speed). Sift flour and cornflour, and gradually blend into egg yolk mixture. Whisk egg whites until stiff but not dry, and fold gently into yolk mixture. Place equal quantities of batter into 3 round 20 cm/8 inch cake tins (buttered and lightly dusted with flour). Bake in a preheated oven (180°C/350°F/Gas 4) for 45 minutes, or until golden brown. Invert layers on wire racks. When cool, loosen edges and remove from pans.

2 To make orange topping: Beat egg, sugar and grated rind of 1 orange together until foamy. Add 25g/1oz sifted flour and juice of 1 orange, and cook in the top of a double saucepan, stirring all the time, until smooth and thick. Cool. Fold in 300ml/½ pint double cream, whipped, reserving some for decoration.

3 Spread two cake layers with some of the orange topping and put cake together. Cover sides of cake with remaining topping and pat chopped toasted almonds firmly around sides. Cover top and decorate with peeled orange segments or chocolate curls.

Pastries

Making pastry is child's play. A good *pâte sablée* (rich shortcrust pastry) is just a combination of flour, butter, sugar and salt and a little cold water and egg yolk to hold it together. Yet the variations on this basic pastry mix - once you have acquired a little know-how - are limitless. I like to serve French savoury tarts as a perfect beginning to a special dinner, or as a main course for a summer luncheon or picnic. The basic pastry can be used for all kinds of savoury tarts and quiches and, with a little more icing sugar added, for rich dessert tarts and flans.

The icing sugar is the secret ingredient here, the catalyst that combines all the other ingredients into a smooth, buttery, crumbly whole.

But remember: there can be no guesswork if you want to make perfect pastry. Use scales and *measuring spoons* for accurate measures; a *measuring jug* for all liquid measurements; a wire pastry blender to blend butter and flour quickly; and an *electric timer* to remind you when to take your pastry out of the oven.

Always use French pastry tins with loose bottoms. Line with dough and bake according to instructions. Then remove fluted ring, leaving tart or flan invisibly supported on loose metal bottom.

Fingertip pastry

My favourite pastry for quicks and tarts is *pâte sablée*, a crumbly pastry which I call *'fingertip' pastry* because it is so rich you literally just press it together in the tart tin.

To make fingertip pastry you need 225g/8oz sifted flour, 125g/5 oz diced butter, 1 tablespoon icing sugar, a little salt to counteract the sweetness of the sugar, an egg yolk and a little iced water.

First, mix the diced butter, sifted flour, sugar and salt with a pastry blender, or with two knives held scissor-fashion, so that the butter can be cut into the flour without the mix getting heavy or greasy. Cut the butter into the flour until the pieces are about pea size, then use your fingers to work the butter further into the flour, lifting your hands high, until the mixture resembles coarse sand.

Combine the egg yolk with an equal amount of iced water, mix well and add to the pastry in the bowl. Now, mix the dough with a spoon (it will be a little more difficult to handle at this point) and when well blended, roll the dough into a ball. Wrap it closely in a clean kitchen towel and put it in the refrigerator for 30 minutes. Fingertip pastry is as easy as that.

To roll out pastry

Flour the working surface so the pastry will not stick to the surface, and flour the rolling pin too. Start rolling out the pastry, always rolling from the centre, turning the dough over occasionally so that the surface is always floured a bit on each side. When rolling out the pastry from the centre, try not to stretch it in any way. If you stretch it - either in rolling it out or in fitting it into the pastry tin - you will find that when baked, it pulls back again into its original shape and leaves the sides of the pastry tin. If the pastry breaks apart or splits while you are handling it, don't worry. Fingertip pastry is so rich a mix that you can patch it up in a second by just pressing it together with your fingers, hence the name, fingertip pastry.

To line pastry tin with pastry

To line the pastry tin, roll the pastry gently over your rolling pin and lift it over the pastry tin. If you are using individual tins, cut rolled out pastry into appropriately sized pieces to cover tins, leaving about 5 cm/ 2 inches to spare. Then ease the pastry gently over the tin (or tins) and press it loosely down into the sides of tin (or tins) using a little too much pastry. Press it against the sides of the pastry tin (or tins) and up, until it is of the thickness required. Then roll your rolling pin quickly across the top of the tin (or tins) to cut off the excess pastry neatly.

Prick the base and sides of your pastry shell (or shells) all over with a fork and chill pastry for 30 minutes in the refrigerator. This rest will minimize the danger of it 'running down' the sides of the tin (or tins) when it is first put into the oven.

To bake pastry

You need a fairly hot oven for pastry. If it is not hot enough the butter will melt and run out before the starch grains in the flour have had time to burst and absorb it. If the oven is too hot, however, the pastry will burn before it has risen properly. When baking pastry, open and close the door as gently as possible and never more often than is absolutely necessary.

If pastry becomes too brown before it has cooked sufficiently, cover it with foil or a double sheet of greaseproof paper that has been lightly sprinkled with water.

To bake blind

The bottom layer of pastry or tarts, quiches or flans that are to contain a creamy or liquid filling can become soggy if they are not half-baked before they are filled. This process is called baking 'blind'.

Line a 20 or 22 ½ cm/8 or 9 inch pastry tin with pastry, fluting the edges if necessary, and chill. Prick bottom with a fork, cover bottom of pastry with a piece of waxed paper or foil, and fill with a layer of dried beans. Bake in a hot oven (230°C/450°F/Gas 8) for about 15 minutes, just long enough to set the crust without browning it. Remove beans and paper or foil and allow to cool. Fill with the desired filling and bake in a moderate oven (190°C/375°F/Gas 5) until cooked. The beans can be reserved in a storage jar and used again.

To bake pastry case only

Bake 'blind' as above for 15 minutes, remove beans and foil. Reduce oven temperature to190°C/375°F/Gas 5 and bake for 10-15 minutes. If crust becomes too brown at edges, cover rim with a little crumpled foil.

French Raspberry Tart

SERVES 4-6

1 23cm/9 inch fingertip pastry case, unbaked (see page 214)
Fresh raspberries, to cover

1 recipe crème pâtissière (see page 220)
1 recipe raspberry fruit glaze (see page 220)

1 Bake prepared pastry case 'blind' in a hot oven (230°C/450°F/Gas 8) for 15 minutes. Reduce oven temperature to 180°C/350°F/Gas 4 and bake for 30 minutes. If crust becomes too brown at edges, cover with a little crumpled foil.

2 Make crème pâtissière.

3 Make raspberry fruit glaze.

4 To assemble tart: Half-fill baked pastry case with crème pâtissière and arrange raspberries in circles on top. Coat with raspberry fruit glaze. Serve chilled.

Moroccan Orange Tart with Dates and Almonds

SERVES 4-6

1 recipe fingertip pastry (see page 214)
1 recipe crème pâtissière (see page 220)

Orange, Almond and Date Topping
4 small oranges
12 dates, pitted and chopped
Apple jelly or greengage conserve, sieved
Slivered almonds

1 Bake prepared pastry case 'blind' in a hot oven (230 C/450 F/Gas 8) for 15 minutes. Reduce oven temperature to 180 C/350F/Gas 4 and bake for 30 minutes. If crust becomes too brown at edges, cover with a little crumpled foil.

2 Make *crème pâtissière*.

3 To assemble tart: Fill baked pastry shell with *crème pâtissière*. Peel 4 small oranges, removing all pith, and slice thinly. Arrange orange slices on top of the flan in an overlapping circle. Fill centre with finely chopped dates.

4 To decorate: Brush orange slices with a little sieved apple jelly or greengage conserve and sprinkle with slivered almonds.

American Chocolate Tarts

SERVES 6

6 individual baked pastry shells (see page 215)

Chocolate Cream
50g/2 oz bitter chocolate
225g/8oz sugar
2 tablespoons cornflour
¼ teaspoon salt
450 ml/¾ pint hot milk

2 eggs, well beaten
4 level tablespoons butter
½ teaspoon vanilla essence

Decoration
300 ml/½ pint double cream
50g/ 2 oz icing sugar
½ teaspoon vanilla essence
Glacé cherries and angelica

1 *To make chocolate cream:* Melt chocolate over hot water in the top of a double saucepan. Combine sugar, cornflour and salt in a bowl and gradually stir in the hot milk. Stir mixture into melted chocolate. Cook over boiling water, stirring constantly, for 10 minutes, or until thick. Pour hot mixture into well-beaten eggs, a little at a time, stirring after each addition. Return to top of double saucepan and cook, stirring occasionally, for 5 minutes. Remove from heat, and add butter and ½ teaspoon vanilla essence.

2 Pour mixture into baked pastry shells.

3 Whip cream and blend in the icing sugar and vanilla essence. Decorate tarts with whipped cream, glacé cherries and angelica. Chill and serve.

Pears in Pastry Sabayon

SERVES 6

6 ripe pears
150ml/¼ pint syrup (made with
   225g/8 oz sugar and 8 tablespoons
   water)
150ml/¼ pint apricot jam for glaze
   (see page 200)
Sabayon sauce or crème fraîche

Pastry
250g/9 oz plain flour

1 teaspoon salt
4 tablespoons lard
100g/4 oz softened butter
Iced water, to mix

Sabayon sauce
4 egg yolks
100g/4 oz sugar
175ml/6 fl oz Marsala
1-2 tablespoons Cognac

To make pastry:
1 Sift flour and salt together. Rub in lard and half the butter until the mixture resembles fine breadcrumbs. Add sufficient water to form into a ball which will just hold together. Knead pastry firmly but quickly until smooth. Rest in a cool place for 30 minutes.

2 Roll out into an oblong and spread remaining butter over the surface. Fold pastry in half, seal edges, rest for 10 minutes in refrigerator and then roll out to 3mm/⅛ inch thickness. Cut pastry rounds, large enough for pears to sit upon, and cut remaining pastry into thin strips using a pastry wheel to give an attractive serrated edge.

To prepare pears:
1 Poach pears in syrup and apricot jam. Cool, and place 1 pear on each pastry round. Preheat oven to 220°C/425°F/Gas 7.

2 Make 'cage' of pastry strips for each pear by crossing 2 pastry strips at right angles. Seal well with water and place 1 pastry cross at top of each pear. Snip pastry strips at base and seal to base with water. Place pears in pastry on baking sheet and bake in preheated oven for 20 minutes or until pastry is golden brown.

3 Remove from oven and brush pears and pastry with apricot fruit glaze. Serve with crème fraîche or sabayon sauce.

To make sabayon sauce:
1 With a hand-held electric mixer whisk egg yolks and sugar in the top of a double saucepan until light and frothy. Whisk in Marsala; place over simmering water and cook, stirring constantly, until sauce is thick and foamy.

2 Stir in Cognac and chill until ready to serve.

Crème Pâtissière

450ml/1 pint milk
5cm/2 inch piece of vanilla pod, split
5 egg yolks
100g/4 oz castor sugar

2 tablespoons plain flour, sifted
1 tablespoon cornflour, sifted
1 tablespoon butter
Few drops of vanilla essence

1 Pour milk into a medium-sized pan and add split vanilla pod. Bring to boiling point over a low heat. Cover pan and put aside to infuse until needed.

2 In a bowl, whisk egg yolks with sugar until thick and light. Gradually whisk in flour and cornflour.

3 Fish vanilla pod out of milk and gradually pour milk into egg yolk mixture, whisking until well blended.

4 Pour mixture back into the pan and bring to the boil over a moderate heat, stirring constantly. Then simmer for 3 minutes longer, beating vigorously.

5 Remove pan from heat; beat in 1 level tablespoon butter and beat a little longer to cool the pastry cream slightly before adding the vanilla essence.

6 Put cream in a bowl and cover with lightly buttered greaseproof paper to prevent a skin forming on top. Allow to become quite cold, then chill until required.

Fruit Glaze

300 ml/½ pint apricot, raspberry
or red currant jam or jelly
Kirsch

Add 4-6 tablespoons water to apricot jam and heat, stirring constantly, until liquid. Flavour to taste with kirsch.

Index

221